Fighting 4
Justice is not
a CRIME!

TALKING BACK

VOICES OF COLOR

Edited and with an introduction by NELLIE WONG

RED LETTER PRESS • Seattle

Red Letter Press
4710 University Way NE, Suite 100
Seattle, WA 98105 • (206)985-4621
RedLetterPress@juno.com
www.RedLetterPress.org

First Edition
ISBN: 978-0-932323-32-3

Book design: Helen Gilbert

Front cover photo: Chicago protest of FBI raids on
anti-war activists, September 2010. (*Fight Back! News*)

Back cover photo: Rally for education, March 2010,
Oakland, California. (*Chris Voss*)

Many articles in this book were first published in
the *Freedom Socialist* newspaper.

Library of Congress Cataloging-in-Publication Data

Talking back : voices of color / edited and with an introduction
by Nellie Wong. – First edition.
     pages cm
  Includes index.
  ISBN 978-0-932323-32-3
  1. Minorities–United States–Social conditions. 2. Minorities–Political
activity–United States. 3. Minority women–United States. 4. Feminism–
United States. I. Wong, Nellie.
  E184.A1T345 2015
  305.800973–dc23
                                    2015001151

1

CONTENTS

4. Sisters doing it

5. Speaking from the heart

6. A global lens

7. Shaking it up

8. In their footsteps

Introduction

Nellie Wong

Talking back? More like no talking back. That's what I was told. In Oakland, California, where I was born and raised, my elders, my teachers, and others in authority drummed it into my compliant ears. Young as I was, through grade school and, yes, even high school, I rarely talked back. Being safe and secure, being what was expected of me as a Chinese female in America, obedience and silence became discomforting siblings in what I deemed was normal.

It was better not to be scolded, not to rankle those who had power over me. Talking back was not for this born-in-the-U.S.A. girl. After all, I'd be set for life. This working woman would get married, have babies. This 8-to-5 secretary would be taken care of, not have to think, not have to make decisions; she could be irresponsible and oh so carefree.

But the voice, long dormant, constricted as it was in my parched throat, fought for freedom, no longer fearful of its sounds, scratchy, discordant, supposedly unfeminine, not reaching the melodies of Cantonese opera that I'd watched as a girl in dark theaters in San Francisco Chinatown. My world split open during the 1970s at San Francisco State University as I listened and read and began opening my mouth and talking back. And especially so when I began writing. In feminist studies, creative writing, English literature and Asian American Studies classes.

In searching for what I thought was only my personal liberation, I discovered a broader reality. I discovered that voices of color, of black, brown, yellow and indigenous, all genders, gay and straight, in all their vibrant hues and tones, gathered together an outer world that was mine as well. The 1960s Third World strikes on college campuses for Native American, Black, Chicano/a, Asian/Pacific, and Women Studies had led the way. The Women Writers Union, which grew out of an intense and organized battle for more women and people-of-color faculty and curriculum, voiced a crying need for the heretofore silenced, ignored and shunted aside. I took the plunge. Now a secretary, now a student, talking back with the cacophony of voices feeding my hungry ears.

Fortunately for me, as I was finding voice I met sisters in Radical Women (RW) and members of the Freedom Socialist Party (FSP) whose analysis of race, sex and class liberation convinced me that organizing to make change was where I belonged. From a muddy, distorted vision as a private individual to a materialist vision as a public activist. From "I can't do anything" humbug to "Yes, we can," sparked the power of voice, at once aural and written, into action — socialist feminism, a vital force for radical social change. This was home.

Talking back was — and is — a potent force, a crucial step in understanding that race oppression, sex discrimination, abusive bosses, income inequality, poverty, homelessness, and never-ending war were systemic, institutionalized under capitalism to wreak havoc on our political, working and creative lives.

In *Talking Back: Voices of Color*, you will find a bounty of voices, an ensemble that brings truth to the floor, shepherded by the National Comrades of Color Caucus (NCCC) of the Freedom Socialist Party and Radical Women.

The NCCC, unique in the U.S. Left, comprises members of color of these two affiliated socialist feminist organizations.

We are Black, Latino/a, Asian/Pacific Islander, Indigenous, of mixed race, LGBTQ, straight, immigrant and U.S.-born, multi-aged, and of different abilities. Together we help each other find our individual and collective voices. We announce them from the muscles and guts of our bodies, from our all-seeing eyes and vibrant ears, understanding the shout-outs born out of rage and hope. We find mutual support as radicals of color working together across race and gender lines. We share histories, food, experiences. We argue, we debate, uniting together with a mighty body of voices for revolutionary change that spans history and the globe.

The Comrades of Color Caucus is a place to put our thoughts, to shape and hone them. An opportunity to become and be leaders. Talking back and out. Our voices singing out for sweet victories that engage and move us forward. Together. This, too, is home.

Most important, we provide FSP and RW with leadership, correction, analysis and proposals for action in the movements and on the issues of people of color. We bring our voices back to the parent organizations, where all are determined to confront racism, empower women and end our oppression as workers. Together, we lay the basis for dismantling U.S. capitalism and building a socialist feminist society where all will not just survive, but thrive.

Exploring ideas and long-hidden histories is also a form of finding voice. Through Revolutionary Integration, a theoretical framework of the FSP, I learned that finding the path to liberation comes from a deep understanding of a people's history and social realities. Revolutionary Integration shows that justice for U.S. Blacks cannot be found through separatism but by a united struggle alongside this country's richly hued working class. And further, African Americans and other people of color — maligned, brutalized and steeled by centuries of resistance – provide irreplaceable leadership for reaching a new day of freedom. So my liberation as an Asian American is bound up with that of Blacks whose battle against racial exploitation and indignity continues to this day.

As a feminist of Chinese American roots, my disrespected skin color and low-paid status as a secretarial worker shocked me into a realization that I've embraced now for many years: the knowledge that racist, sexist, anti-queer, anti-trans, anti-worker discrimination leveled against one is leveled against all. We must seek integration into revolutionary change, not into a business-as-usual capitalist America that puts people of color and women in chains. That's what's necessary.

Through this collection, readers are given a rare jewel: a gem ablaze with the colors of working-class voices, rather than abstractions from lofty academic towers. The offerings by FSP and RW members of color and activist allies speak out with deepest respect and understanding for the essential work in the multi-issued movements. The fight for quality public education, reproductive justice and freedom of expression, and an end to police violence and war – this and much more is contained in this volume.

To whom do we talk back? To those who will silence us. Those who incarcerate us in prison or in the home. Those who deny us our rights to cross borders to seek refuge from violence and safety for our children. Those who brutalize us because of our race, gender or sexuality. Those who dictate rigid male-female identities rather than acknowledge the full human palette of gender. Those who attack unions and deny working women and men the right to organize, to strike. Those who destroy the environment, causing pollutants that make people sick. And much more. These voices of color matter. They need to be heard. Everywhere. That's why this collection is important. It's born in and outside of the home, on the streets, at workplaces and battlefields.

As James Baldwin, celebrated Black gay author and activist, has said:

> You write in order to change the world.... If you alter, even by a millimeter, the way people look at reality, then you can change it.

That's our goal beginning with talking back.

San Francisco, California

1. READING, WRITING — RESISTANCE!

The fight for working-class education at City College of San Francisco

Duciana Thomas

Education has always been important to me. Going to school in the low-income Bayview district of San Francisco, which is mostly people of color, I saw firsthand the hopelessness of young people from working-class families with no resources. I also saw the amazing difference that programs such as Head Start made by providing preschool for poor children.

Education should be a right for everyone. But the withholding of public funds is making it something only for the privileged. College administrations are raising fees, cutting programs, and shrinking staff. Without financial aid, working-class and poor students become less likely to attend college, or get an Associate of Arts degree, or transfer to a university.

What's happening at City College of San Francisco (CCSF) is a good example of national attacks on public higher education. City College, which serves more than 85,000 working-class students who are predominantly of color, has been threatened with loss of accreditation due to false accusations of "deficiencies." Due to these attacks, it has shed more than 5,000 students. Diversity-related departments, such as African American and LGBT Studies, risk being eliminated. Noncitizen students now have to pay nonresident tuition — an increase of thousands of dollars. Programs geared towards working-class students have also been cut with the loss of funding.

One of the learning services that was eliminated was called the Gender Diversity Project. We made presentations on campus about the importance of safety for transgender and non-gender-conforming students. The class was such a success in discussing safety that many stayed in the group after they were no longer paid. What City College used to have, the inherent essence of what has changed so many lives for those who were able to attend, was that it was quality, affordable, public education — inclusive to the working-class community in the Bay Area. Due to these cuts and attacks, that which made City College has been damaged.

Joining the fight to save CCSF

In March of 2013, I found myself marching side by side with Radical Women in a Bay Area protest against the threats to City College. Radical Women and Freedom Socialist Party worked together to publicize the privatization of education, including City College, and to create a strong defense of students, faculty, and union members to fight for the school in the Save CCSF Coalition. Radical Women members and I immediately connected because we were equally passionate about the attacks on affordable and public education. Radical Women's priority was to motivate women of color and other students of color to take on leadership roles in this struggle because they were going to be the most affected. We wanted to connect students, faculty, and the community. City College of San Francisco had changed the lives of so many people, we knew the presence of the surrounding community was needed at the forefront of the fight.

It is working-class students of color who have the most difficult time integrating class schedules with busy work demands and who will lose out if Ethnic and Women's Studies' classes are eliminated. It is working-class women of color who will suffer most if childcare programs are shut down.

Radical Women decided to put on a campus workshop where women of color in Ethnic, Women's, and Gender Studies could hear the perspective of three women of color leading in the CCSF fight. By educating about the damage being done to City College, the negative effects of privatization for women of color, and the need for people to step up, we hoped to inspire women of color to take on leadership in this movement.

> We as a community refuse to allow our schools to be taken from us or attacks to diminish us.

The workshop turned out great. Women's Studies classes came, plus union-based faculty from Save CCSF, and some very enthusiastic students. Students talked about being first-generation immigrants and how necessary it was for them that tuition stay affordable. Others raised how committed they were to being able to complete programs such as nursing.

The next focus of our work was for Radical Women and Save CCSF to participate in the annual March in March, where students from all over California travel to Sacramento to rally for education issues. We decided to go one step further with a post-march rally in front of the office of State Chancellor Brice Harris.

We made announcements on campus in classes filled with eager women and students of color. We pushed the unions to participate and tried to feel out the student government to see what it was planning. Unfortunately, the administration and student government support for the March in March turned out to be much less than in previous years.

Regardless, Radical Women and the passionate Save CCSF crew of faculty, staff, and students headed to Sacramento. We passed out flyers and then headed to the post-rally demonstration. We proudly marched in front of Brice

Harris's office and made such a noise that he begrudgingly agreed to meet with us! Our determination and excitement put a shocked look on his face that I will never forget. We told him to stop the privatization. We said we didn't need the special trustee who was implementing policies to close down the school. We demanded democratic decisions. He was surprised by how knowledgeable we were.

Harris had nothing but evasive political responses but his shock at our understanding of the issues made the whole day worthwhile.

From these experiences, I have learned the need to meet students where they are at. If you reach out to them, you'll find that they might not be able to do everything but they can do something.

People like to get mad. But they don't like to get scared. And a lot of people are scared at City College. We have to give them answers and say you don't have to be afraid. You just have to get up and do something.

Learning from history

At Radical Women's Black History Month celebration this year we watched a film on the Little Rock Nine, the courageous Black youths who desegregated Central High School in Arkansas in 1957. We talked about the parallels between the fight against race segregation then and what's going on now to save City College. It was heartbreaking to realize that the struggles were eerily similar. I was watching these young Black students trying to get an education — obviously determined and passionate about getting an education — yet this literal wall of racism — a wall that they were standing against formed by a crowd outside the school yelling obscenities and racial slurs — was keeping them from it. On the other hand, it was inspiring because the looks on their faces revealed a determination that could not be broken. In that moment, in

Nancy Reiko Kato

Nearly 1,000 students, faculty and community members protest the threat to shut down City College of San Francisco in March 2013.

that night, I finally realized that CCSF wasn't just important to me; I finally realized how important it was to everyone — past and present.

The Little Rock students were fervently dedicated to getting an education and stayed determined to get it. They broke through the wall and ended up going to that school, despite obstacles.

The fight for CCSF has just begun. We have won against some very damaging attacks but they are still coming. However, similar to those Little Rock students, the CCSF faculty, staff, students, and community members are staying strong in keeping the message clear about the importance of the school. We as a community refuse to allow our school to be taken from us, we refuse to allow these walls or attacks to diminish us, and we will continue to face the problematic changes being implemented on our school. City College belongs to us and though the fight for it will be tough, we will not stand down.

The unfinished battle for quality public schools

Yuisa Gimeno

))) I was born and raised in Boston and am a product of its public school system. I'm also the daughter of working-class immigrants and was raised by a single mom.

She fought hard for my brother and me, especially for our right to a decent, respectful and quality education.

For women, especially women of color, access to education is a life-and-death issue like the right to abortion, birth control and healthcare. Their availability influences our life choices and our ability to be economically and socially independent.

Education helps narrow the wage gap for those able to graduate from high school, college or graduate school. And gaining access to our own history inspires oppressed people to organize against racism, sexism, homophobia and other forms of bigotry.

Parents along with teachers and students should have control over the content and quality of education students receive.

Origins of the U.S. education system

Contrary to popular belief, the public education system wasn't a favor from the bosses or their politician friends. No, our class — the working class — fought and organized for this right. W.E.B. Du Bois properly credits and shows in great detail in his book *Black Reconstruction in America* that freed Black slaves organized the first true public education system in the U.S.:

The first great mass movement for public education at the expense of the state, in the South, came from Negroes. Many leaders before the war had advocated general education, but few had been listened to.... Some states had elaborate plans, but they were not carried out. Public education for all at public expense was, in the South, a Negro idea.

Du Bois describes the *political* purpose of public education as being to help "poor, degraded and disadvantaged" former slaves to

...develop some...necessary social leadership; to seek the right sort of leadership from other groups; to strive for increase of knowledge, so as to teach themselves wisdom and the rhythm of united effort.

I agree. Public education is about developing leadership and uniting the working class in order to change society from the bottom up. The current battle for quality public schools is the legacy of this fight.

Slavery, Reconstruction and post-Reconstruction

During slavery, it was illegal for slaves to be taught how to read or write. Nevertheless, they and their teachers — Black and white — risked their lives for the sake of knowledge.

After the Civil War, the Reconstruction era began. It was a revolutionary period: the right to vote was extended to Black men and poor white men. Blacks were elected to local and state government positions and freed slaves organized the first public schools open to everyone.

By 1867, 191 day schools and 45 night schools were reported in Georgia. These successes were mirrored in Louisiana, North Carolina, Mississippi and other Southern states.

However, by 1877, Reconstruction was brutally smashed in a racist counter-revolution that was abetted by Northern white capitalists. Federal troops pulled out. Former slave owners and Confederate politicians were determined to prevent freed Black slaves and poor white sharecroppers from finding unity through fighting together for public education and jobs. Mobs of angry whites destroyed schools and physically attacked both white and Black teachers. Many of the mobs were led by the Ku Klux Klan.

The press fueled hostility towards white teachers and played on racial fears and the myth of Black inferiority. Taxes for funding schools were eliminated. African Americans were outraged. Du Bois writes:

> When the collection of the general tax for Negro schools was suspended in Louisiana by military order, the colored people were greatly aroused and sent in petitions. One of these petitions, thirty feet in length, represented ten thousand Negroes....

Despite heroic resistance, Southern education regressed to mostly educating whites with only a fraction of funding going for Black students.

Forced segregation became the law in the South, with de facto segregation in the North. In California, laws were passed that mandated that Mexican children — U.S.-born or not — were not allowed to go to school with whites. Racially divided schools, housing and jobs led to a lower standard of living for everybody.

The civil rights movement rose in revolt over these conditions. By the 1960s, battles to integrate public schools were raging.

The struggle still continues

Achieving integrated, quality public education has revolutionary aspects. It requires total equality based on economic and social gains that would benefit the entire working class.

So it's important to help people see that current attacks on education and social services are assaults on all workers and require a fight-back led by unions, Blacks, other people of color and women.

Here in California, Governor Brown and the bipartisan legislature intend to shred education and services rather than end 30 years of tax breaks for big business. They want to use public money for private charter schools. To do this, they need to break the education unions and other public employee unions. Instead of fair taxes on big business, they want to steal workers' pensions.

Students who fall behind get a pass into the prison system, fueling the school-to-prison pipeline.

Many school policies are designed to produce a non-union, compliant labor force. And students who fall behind get a pass into the prison system, fueling the school-to-prison pipeline that is so injurious to youth of color.

Attacks on public education are part of a neoliberal economic policy that the U.S. and international capitalist institutions are imposing all over the world. Public funding for education comes from the taxes paid by workers and from the taxes paid by bosses on the profits we generate for them. When education and other public resources are privatized, it is a wholesale transfer of the public wealth into private hands for the sake of individual profit. Not just education but parks, water, electricity, and libraries are under threat.

To prop up capitalism, the bosses and politicians from both parties are driving down the standard of living for the 99 percent and keeping the profits for themselves. In order to do this, they need to break the back of the labor movement. Undermining quality education, attacking the teachers unions, and eliminating affirmative action are part of this onslaught.

How to defend public education

The movement for schools must demand quality, integrated public education for all — regardless of immigration status. We must defend and support the leadership of women and people of color, who are in the forefront against cuts to education and other social services because they are hardest hit. We must push the labor movement and our communities to: 1) oppose charter schools; 2) defend teachers and other school workers; 3) support libraries and a broad-based curriculum including arts and Ethnic Studies; 4) demand that schools and social services be funded through taxes on the rich and corporations; 5) support immediate, unconditional legalization of undocumented workers with full rights to services and education; and 6) dump the Democratic Party which, like the Republican Party, is overseeing the neoliberal attack on schools and services.

To those who say this program is too ambitious, I reply: Look at the women workers of Egypt who helped topple their government in 18 days. Look at the student and worker strikers at the University of Puerto Rico who ended the police occupation of their campus and stopped tuition hikes. Look at the history of the fight for education in the U.S.

If our sisters and brothers succeeded under those extreme conditions, then we can win this fight. We owe it to them, to ourselves and to our class.

"Reverse discrimination" cases further threaten school integration

Annaliza Torres

Two "reverse discrimination" school cases brought before the U.S. Supreme Court have taken the country closer to the complete elimination of affirmative action. The cases, brought by parents of white students in Washington State and Kentucky, were bids to bar the use of race as any kind of factor in determining which schools K-12 students attend.

They are part of a chain of attacks on affirmative action that are accompanied by severe cuts in school funding that have caused people in 45 states to sue those states for failing to provide enough money for basic education. This miserly funding contributes to growing inequality in the schools. Schools in poorer neighborhoods where people of color predominate, which have never had the resources of schools in better-off, mostly white areas, are struggling more than ever.

Why affirmative action is needed

In Louisville, the parent of a 5-year-old sued the Jefferson County Board of Education after her son's transfer request to a preferred kindergarten closer to his home was denied in 2002.

In Seattle, the parents of a first-year high school student founded a parent organization that sued the school district after their daughter failed to be placed at Ballard High in 2000. Ballard, the most popular high school in the city, boasts a renovated facility, offers unique programs such as a biotech academy and maritime institute, and was also the closest to the student's home.

In both Louisville and Seattle, competition for the most desired schools is fierce, and students may not get their top choice for a variety of reasons — race among them.

The economics of ongoing racism work against integrated neighborhoods and integration of schools.

In Louisville, racial diversity is factored into the admissions mix upfront. In Seattle, it was one thing that could be considered as a tie-breaker when too many students apply for the same school.

Despite the Supreme Court's anti-segregation ruling in *Brown v. Board of Education of Topeka* in 1954, schools in Louisville remained separated by color until a federal judge ordered a desegregation program in 1975. When the schools were declared sufficiently integrated nearly 25 years later, the county board decided to continue to use race-conscious criteria to keep them that way. The school district is one of the most integrated in the country.

Seattle was the first large city to adopt desegregation strategies, including mandatory busing, without a federal court order. But with passage of a state anti-affirmative action initiative looming in the late 1990s, the district dropped busing, though it clung to a sliver of commitment to diversity with its use of race in tie-breaking.

In implementing the *Brown* decision, busing became an explosive issue across the U.S. Some opponents were racists. Others were parents, including Black parents, who objected to the sometimes long distances children had to travel and the additional burden placed on parents who wanted to participate in school affairs.

The organic way to achieve integration of schools would be through integrated neighborhoods. But the economics of ongoing racism works against that, with African Americans and other people of color still vastly overrepresented in the poor sections of town and whites still predominant in most well-off areas. Plain discrimination in renting, selling, and granting loans and mortgages entrenches the division.

As long as these inequalities persist, affirmative action is necessary.

Everyone's stake in integration

On December 4, 2006, the Supreme Court heard arguments from the Louisville and Seattle school districts, defending their policies, and the parents and the Bush administration, seeking to overturn them.

Those were not the only voices heard that day. Students, civil rights activists, feminists, and others traveled to Washington, D.C., from around the country to take part in a spirited rally in support of integration and affirmative action. Organized largely by BAMN (Coalition to Defend Affirmative Action and Immigrant Rights and Fight for Equality By Any Means Necessary), it was endorsed by groups from the NAACP and NOW to the American Federation of Teachers and the national YWCA, with Howard University students as its backbone.

Groups and individuals including the NAACP, the National Women's Law Center, Latino organizations, and members of Congress also submitted briefs to the court supporting the school districts. Nevertheless, in June 2007, the court ruled 5-4 that achieving racial diversity could *not* be a factor in school admissions.

This left unresolved not only the problem of equal opportunities for kids of color, but also the problem of providing a quality public education for all.

Integration, in and of itself, was never the answer for improving education for kids of color. Sitting next to a white student doesn't make you better educated — but being in smaller classes, with more attention from teachers and with access to computers and to art, music, and language classes, probably will. But these things are vanishing for all children, at the same time that resurgent racism is making integration in every part of life more important.

Good schools should offer chances to be exposed to different people and experiences, not just to achieve high test scores and learn fancier techniques for competing at the workplace. Quality education must be redefined and tailored to benefit real, whole children, not the capitalist employers who will someday exploit them as workers. Students of color and all children deserve a holistic, racially integrated public educational system that appreciates different cultures and languages and includes studies in the history of oppression and resistance.

Schools like this can only be maintained by community control, with administrators educationally and financially accountable to local communities. And they must be generously funded. Instead of taxing homeowners and obliging parents to fundraise, funding should come from the bottomless military budget and taxes on big business.

In class terms, the value of integrated learning environments is that they can go a long way toward breaking down barriers of prejudice and hostility. They can be important paving stones on the road toward working-class solidarity — the missing ingredient for challenging the profit system that so stifles the human potential of children today.

Are charter schools the answer to inequality in public education?

Lillian Thompson

"Charter school"...what comes to mind when these words are uttered?

According to the National Education Association (NEA), a charter school is "a primary or secondary school that receives public money but is not subject to some of the rules, regulations and statutes that apply to public schools, in exchange for some type of accountability for producing certain results, which are set forth in each school's charter."

Parents of color are encouraged to believe that charter schools are the panacea to the obstacles their children face due to institutional racism and underfunding in the public schools. But are charter schools truly the answer to inequality in schools? No! The truth must be exposed to stop these for-profit organizations.

Two-tier education, union-busting, lower living standards

Charter schools actually hinder the development of students of color in several ways, while at the same time eroding the quality of public education.

First, they increase classroom segregation by race. In 2010, the UCLA Civil Rights Project released a study showing that seven of ten Black charter school students attend schools with extremely low numbers of white students. It also

found that 32 percent of charter school students are Black —
twice the percentage as in public schools.

These schools aggravate other kinds of segregation as
well. They gain access to lists of high-achieving students
and poach them from public schools. They cherry-pick their
students with a restrictive enrollment application and are
legally allowed to reject students with special needs: those
with physical or cognitive disabilities, for example, or English
language learners. What's even more appalling is that this
exclusion is done with taxpayers' money! Publicly funded
schools should be required to serve the needs of *all* children
— not just the ones with the best chance of success.

Charters are also the trigger for union-busting. Teachers'
unions, longtime defenders of quality schools, have to be
silenced in order for public schools to be closed and replaced
with charters. Most charter school teachers have no union representation and can be terminated for any reason as long as the decision is not based illegally on a characteristic like age, race or sex.

Charter schools are the trigger for union-busting and segregation by race, language and ability.

Imagine working under that kind of pressure with 40 students *or more* in a classroom! This helps to explain why the average teacher in a charter school works there for less than five years.

Public school teachers are required to have earned a
bachelor's degree and gone through a student teaching
program. Charter school teachers are not. The American
Federation of Teachers (AFT) and the NEA are two unions
that were created to ensure that educators would have rights
as professionals, health benefits, and wages *above* the minimum.

Children will suffer and living standards of U.S. workers

will drop if the teachers' unions are broken and a two-tier educational system takes hold.

Education for the masses!

Originally, freed slaves — defying threats to their lives — established the public education system in the South as a tool to empower disenfranchised African Americans and to create equal educational opportunities for all people. I vehemently defend public education because I myself am a successful product of the Los Angeles Unified School District, the second-largest public school system in the nation!

With encouragement from my family and some very hard-working, dedicated teachers, I beat the odds in spite of my humble beginnings.

Had charter schools been around when I was growing up, I would *not* have been able to attend due to their selective rules. Many require a minimum of two hours per week of on-site parent volunteer service. That would have eliminated me because my dad worked two jobs to support the family. Charters also often require that parents provide lunch daily for their children. Once again I would have been excluded. And the uniform requirement? I again would have been left out; my mom sewed my clothes because there was no money to buy them.

Would I have been missing out on a stellar education? Probably not.

In 2009, the Center for Research on Educational Outcomes (Stanford University) presented a study comparing charter schools and public schools. Charter schools outperformed public schools only about 17 percent of the time. Nearly 46 percent of charter schools are on par with public schools. However, about 37 percent of charters are rated academically lower. Other factors being fairly equal, how is it possible to start with the "cream of the crop" and yet produce sour milk more than a third of the time?!

Charter schools have sprung up rapidly in New Orleans, New York, Georgia, California, and elsewhere. We need to fight against this destructive wave of ineptitude that charter schools have initiated.

Antidote: united defense of public education

Quality public schools can be an effective road out of a cycle of poverty. They can reduce social inequality, help youngsters achieve their potential, and provide good union jobs for people who care about children. So, how do we fight for them?

Our unions must once again strive to build solidarity with the community — where parents of color are often in the lead. We can also take a giant step in fighting back by participating in ongoing campaigns.

One opportunity for involvement is with Save Our Schools (SOS). SOS demands include equitable funding for all public school communities; an end to high stakes testing used for the purpose of student, teacher, and school evaluation; teacher, family, and community leadership in forming public education policies; and curriculum developed for and by local school communities.

As the famous and deservedly popular anti-war slogan has it, "It will be a great day when our schools get all the money they need, and the Air Force has to hold a bake sale to buy a bomber!"

Standing up for Ethnic Studies: Talks with Rodolfo Acuña and Roberto Rodríguez

Yolanda Alaniz

The ink was barely dry on Arizona's anti-immigrant Senate Bill 1070 requiring racial profiling by police when Governor Jan Brewer signed House Bill 2281 in May 2010. The bill, which took effect at the end of the year, banned any courses that "promote resentment toward a race or class of people," "are designed primarily for pupils of a particular ethnic group," "advocate ethnic solidarity instead of the treatment of pupils as individuals" — or advocate overthrow of the government! In practice, it outlawed Ethnic Studies.

Tom Horne authored the bill while an official with the state Department of Education. Upon becoming attorney general, he immediately declared the Mexican American Ethnic Studies program (Raza Studies) in Tucson's K-12 school district to be illegal. A legal challenge was launched to defend this successful program, which had lowered the high school dropout rate and increased college enrollment.

Horne thinks students should be taught that the U.S. is the "land of opportunity" and "should not be taught that they are oppressed." He objected to the association of Raza Studies with MEChA, a Chicana/o student organization.

In response to this assault, a group of educators, students and community members formed Save Ethnic Studies (SES). Richard Martínez, attorney for SES, filed a complaint charg-

ing that the new law was unconstitutional. As of January 2015, no decision had been issued.

Two professors active in Save Ethnic Studies are Dr. Rodolfo F. Acuña and Roberto "Dr. Cintli" Rodríguez. Acuña, who teaches Chicano Studies at California State University at Northridge, authored the groundbreaking work Occupied America: A History of Chicanos, which is one of Horne's special targets. Rodríguez, who teaches in Mexican American Studies at the University of Arizona, was arrested with students while protesting HB 2281.

The two educators were interviewed separately by Yolanda Alaniz, co-author with Megan Cornish of Viva la Raza: A History of Chicano Identity and Resistance.

Get active, build a movement

Alaniz — *Why is teaching Ethnic Studies important?*
Acuña — It is a vehicle to motivate students of color and poor students to learn. Teaching about historical events is an important motivation to read or write.

Alaniz — *What needs to be done to defend Ethnic Studies?*
Acuña — Help raise money; Richard Martínez is trying to raise a half million dollars to fight this in the courts. Mobilize the grass roots, have house parties, and write letters of support.

Mass action is important, but we have to build a movement. I urge people to join organizations that educate on Marxism and dialectical critical thinking. We can't be complacent — we must see the class interest.

We are defying stereotypes because we want to control our society. The fight in Arizona is one of having a stake in our government and democracy. Students want a say in their education.

Alaniz — *Why is Horne targeting your book and why is this happening now?*

Acuña — During 1963 to 1965 we faced certain problems — the dropout rate and need for bilingual education. We won reforms, including bilingual education and affirmative action. These reforms have been slowly taken away, and the last reform of the 1960s to be taken away is Chicano Studies.

Why now? We cannot underestimate Arizona politics. David and Charles Koch, the American Chamber of Commerce and the National Socialist Movement (Nazi Party) control Arizona politicians, the Tea Party and paramilitary groups. Emulating their draconian tactics in Arizona, the Koch brothers have moved to establish a beachhead in the state of Wisconsin, where they have launched a campaign of fear. The difference is that collective bargaining rights for public workers in Wisconsin have replaced the undocumented worker as the scapegoat. It comes down to economics.

Why my book? One of the reasons is the title. Horne does not recognize that America applies to Latin America! To South America and even Mexico. *Occupied America* begins with Europeans coming to these lands.

An attack on the concept of education

Alaniz — *Is there a comparison between what happened in Nazi Germany and what is happening now with HB 2281 and attacks on immigrants?*

Rodríguez — No, I don't think so. The real story is not all of that stuff. The real story is the leadership that is developing as a result. People are focusing on the Neanderthal 19th century legislation, but what is missing in the media is the story of resistance which is beyond awesome. Not a day goes by without something happening.

When the governor signed HB 2281 into law, over 1,000 middle school and high school students walked out. A whole series of actions have taken place, from forums and marches to the building takeovers that resulted in arrests. One of the most amazing things was the 13-mile walk organized by high school students from one end of Tucson to the other.

Despite all the bad, the good is that all of a sudden we have leadership. I think there has been a vacuum of leadership for many, many years in both Phoenix and Tucson. But now you are talking about dozens upon dozens of youngsters who can speak for themselves.

Michelle and Nancy are examples of two main leaders. Michelle's father was picked up by the FBI — supposedly for bank robbery, but this was just an excuse to get him and hand him over to the *migra*. Now he is in detention. Nancy's father was picked up during the Raza Studies conference in July. It is radicalizing the students because it is their own parents being picked up.

Alaniz — *Were Michelle and Nancy's parents targeted because they are student leaders?*
Rodríguez — It's a question of adding two and two together.

Alaniz — *Would you compare this to the Chicano movement of the 1960s and '70s?*
Acuña — You can draw parallels. Or see it simply as a continuity.

These students have been in Ethnic Studies classes and they have been taught to defend themselves. They value who they are, what they have benefited from, and most of all are aware of their role in creating change. They are part of a culture of creation/resistance.

Alaniz — *Have you gotten solidarity from other communities of color?*
Acuña — Yes, we have it across the board from all communi-

ties, but it could be more.

People who have consciousness understand that when they attack one they attack all of us. Once you have a precedent that certain things are not to be taught in school, you have a grand inquisitor, and that is what we have literally with this law. Some bureaucrat will be approving what is acceptable curriculum, what are acceptable books.

This is not an attack on people of color or on Raza Studies but on the *concept* of education — a narrowing of what can be taught, what is acceptable knowledge. There is nothing wrong with learning about Western civilization, but students should learn everything and anything. We teach them about social justice, about how to be good human beings. Maybe this is what they object to!

2. Crimes of Punishment

Ferguson grand jury props up a rotten, racist system

Statement by the National Comrades of Color Caucus

On Monday, November 24, 2014 St. Louis County Prosecuting Attorney Robert McCulloch announced the verdict that many had feared but expected: Ferguson cop Darren Wilson would not be indicted for the murder of 18-year-old Michael Brown. The failure to level a single charge against Wilson for shooting an unarmed Black teenager caused universal outrage at the utter disregard for the lives of African Americans. Instead, the police, as protectors of property in a system where wealth is the highest virtue, were given a free hand to commit state-sanctioned murder against those who are not rich or white.

Grand jury whitewash

McCulloch's sole shred of hard evidence was a reference to "Brown's DNA found on the inside of the police car," a fact that could mean countless possible scenarios. He said the grand jury concluded from this that Brown's killing was justified — no matter that it happened later and dozens of feet from the car. This logic is full of gaps, yet McCulloch, an elected Democrat, asked the public to simply accept his opinion. Though supposedly Wilson's prosecutor, McCulloch had a strong reason to favor him: the prosecutor's father was a policeman killed in the line of duty.

Like the U.S. justice system as a whole, the grand jury process is deeply flawed. Grand juries take place in total secrecy and without a judge. No lawyer was allowed to represent Brown. The prosecutor runs the show. There is no public scrutiny and no opportunity for lawyers to question the accused or review evidence.

Historically, people of color, leftists, the poor, and women suffer a 98 percent indictment rate when they face a grand jury. But police are almost never indicted.

A class and race divide

Racism is a capitalist invention, created to justify the unconscionable enslavement of an entire people. When slavery was overthrown, racism remained because capitalism uses the lie of inferiority to pay people of color less, and to divide the U.S. working class so it won't rise up against the bosses who grow rich off the labor of others. To prevent revolt, the system uses brutal repression, from public lynchings to today's "lawful" police executions and harassment.

In communities like Ferguson, the poor, who are mostly Black, face unrelenting discrimination from police through mechanisms such as high levels of traffic stops that trigger unaffordable fines, jail sentences for non-payment, suspended licenses, and lost jobs due to arrests. This adds to the severe economic gap between whites and Blacks in Ferguson — where 16 percent of the Black labor force was unemployed from 2010-2012, compared to 8.5 percent of the white labor force.

There is also the constant threat of being killed for driving, walking or shopping "while Black." A person of African American descent is killed by U.S. police every 36 hours. Two-thirds of those killed are younger than 31.

The establishment's defenders are terrified that they won't be able to stop increased revolt in response to the slew of recent police killings of African Americans: Eric Garner, killed by police chokehold on July 17 in Staten Island; John Crawford III killed at a Dayton, Ohio Walmart on August 5 for holding a toy gun; Ezell Ford, killed by Los Angeles police on August 11; Tanesha Anderson, suffering from mental illness, died from injuries when police attacked her in Cleveland on November 12; Akai Gurley, killed when a cop "accidentally" discharged his gun in Brooklyn on November 20; 12-year-old Tamir Rice, fatally shot in Cleveland on November 22 for holding a toy gun at a playground. This litany does not even include recent police violence against other people of color and immigrants.

Militarization of police

With income disparity and protest on the rise, it's no wonder that cops are embracing military-style tanks and weaponry to smash anger and resentment. The well-funded, national militarization of the police is setting the stage for continued mass arrests and escalating crackdowns on resistance to a murderous system. Such tactics are being used by regimes around the world. Closest to home, the U.S. has funded the militarization of the Mexican police who are responsible for the disappearance and presumed deaths of 43 student activists in September 2014.

In anticipation of Ferguson protests, robo-cop encampments were stationed in U.S. cities, especially where sympathy actions were expected. The goal was to intimidate protest. But community members were not deterred. Neither were they dissuaded by Prosecutor McCulloch, President Obama and other Democratic Party "leaders" who demanded protesters be peaceful while failing to warn police to do the same.

We won't be silent

From coast to coast over several days, thousands of people of all races came out to condemn the Ferguson decision, expose local police attacks, and denounce a skewed justice establishment. Black women and youth in Ferguson have played a key role in mobilizing the national response.

How can outrage be focused to end the deaths and overhaul a racist injustice system?

• Call for elected, independent civilian review boards over the police with the right to hire, fire, investigate and discipline.

• Demand the demilitarization of police.

• Call on President Obama to initiate federal charges and bring Darren Wilson to trial.

• Break with Democrats, Republicans and the capitalist system. Work to create a socialist world where meeting human needs, overcoming historic discrimination, and ending systemic violence are the highest priorities.

Who is Assata Shakur, and why is she on the FBI list of top terrorists?

Nellie Wong

))) After three decades in exile as an author and editor in Cuba, Assata Shakur was stigmatized by her longtime predator, the FBI, by becoming the first woman on the Most Wanted Terrorists list in May 2013. The FBI upped the bounty on her head to $2 million! Shakur never was and is not now a terrorist. But the FBI appears desperate to intensify its police-state activities and discredit political dissidents, especially Black revolutionaries.

The frame-up

Shakur was shot twice and arrested in a traffic stop in 1973 on the New Jersey Turnpike for a "faulty tail light." The incident led to a shoot-out that killed a state trooper along with the car's driver, a close friend. Sundiata Acoli, the third companion in the car, was wounded and captured. He remains in prison today.

The trial was a mockery. Her jury was all white. Even after state trooper James Harper testified that he never saw Shakur with a gun and that she was shot while holding up her arms, she and Acoli, both unarmed, were convicted in 1977 of murdering trooper Werner Foerster — and their comrade Zayd Shakur! Assata served time in a men's prison where she was subjected to vaginal and anal strip searches and under continuous threat as a "cop killer." She was able to finally escape with outside help in 1979, and in 1984 fled to Cuba, which gave her political asylum. Radical Women organized the International Feminist Brigade to Cuba in 1997 which met with Shakur and heard her speak.

The making of a radical

Shakur's own experiences shaped her becoming a revolutionary feminist. Her book, *Assata: An Autobiography,* published in 1987, reveals that journey with passion and eloquence. She was raised by loving and strict grandparents who repeatedly told her to "Hold that head up!" and "Who's better than you?" As a Black woman worker, she formed an acute sense of racist and sexist bigotry on the job.

Like many others, Shakur first thought the U.S. was fighting for democracy in Vietnam. But Blacks were being assaulted and killed in her own country. Acquaintances looked down on poor Blacks and were more concerned with making money, buying stuff, and aiming for the so-called American Dream. But Shakur always spoke up for the afflicted and took abuse from nobody. Her quest for personal dignity transformed her into a freedom fighter.

Life in "amerika"

During the 1960s and 1970s tumultuous protest erupted, led first by the Black civil rights struggle, morphing into a militant anti-Vietnam War movement, and deepening to include radical movements for the rights of Chicanos/as, Asian Americans, Native Americans, women, lesbians and gays, disabled people, and Ethnic Studies education.

By 1969, the Black Panther Party had become the number one organization targeted by the FBI's COINTELPRO (Counter Intelligence Program). Any radicals, but particularly Blacks, who spoke out and organized against racial injustice, poverty and war caught the attention of this infamous counter-insurgency plan, which persecuted, framed and assassinated African American militant leaders. The FBI spied on, slandered, and disrupted many U.S. political organizations, including the American Indian Movement, Southern Christian Leadership Conference, NAACP, and Congress of Racial Equality.

During that same time, Assata was involved with the Black Panther Party in New York and the Black Liberation Army. She visited the Oakland branch of the Panthers and sought out Asian brothers and sisters struggling against racism. She concluded that Black nationalism was a dead end; her world view became internationalist.

Government forces brand Shakur as a terrorist because she dares to speak the truth about political repression.

Between 1971 and 1973, she was being hunted down and put on trial for seven different crimes. All of them were dismissed or she was acquitted, once with a hung jury. In 1973, in a compelling opening statement when she and codefendant Ronald Myers stood accused of a bank robbery in 1971 in Queens, New York, Shakur spoke out:

> This case is just another example of what has been going on in this country. Throughout amerika's history, people have been imprisoned because of their political beliefs and charged with criminal acts in order to justify that imprisonment. Those who dared to speak out against the injustices in this country, both Black and white, have paid dearly for their courage, sometimes with their lives.

Thirty years later, government forces would still rather see Shakur dead because she dares to speak the truth about political repression. As the National Conference of Black Lawyers points out, branding her as a terrorist creates an atmosphere the government could conveniently use to justify an assassination.

Says Guerry Hoddersen, former Student Nonviolent Coordinating Committee worker and International Secretary of the Freedom Socialist Party:

> This coming August for the 50th anniversary of the March on Washington, Obama and all the other establishment types will hail Martin Luther King — a dead hero — but say nothing about a living Black woman who fought for justice and socialism, and is now placed on the FBI's top terrorist list. "Amerika" likes its Black heroes dead. It looks back and hails the foresight and courage of those now passed, while burying the living.

An unfinished fight

Today, King's dream for Black America is still far from reality. In June 2013, the Supreme Court struck down the heart of the Voting Rights Act of 1965. This means that racial and ethnic minorities and low-income majorities will face bigger barriers to voting in states with a history of bias. Texas, for example, will put into immediate effect a voter I.D. law that had been blocked by the Voting Rights Act.

Many of the surviving '60s and '70s radicals are still fighting, like the towering political prisoners Mumia Abu-Jamal and Sundiata Acoli. Black women are organizing across the country against massive dismantling of public schools and other social services. Black prisoners were leaders in the momentous, multiracial work and hunger strike of thousands of inmates against solitary confinement and criminal prison abuse that began July 8, 2013.

In a 1998 "Open Letter from Assata," posted by *Colorlines* in May 2013, the 65-year-old revolutionary told her story:

I am a 20th century escaped slave. Because of government persecution, I was left with no other choice than to flee from the political repression, racism and violence that dominate the U.S. government's policy towards people of color. ...Black people, poor people in the U.S. have no real freedom of speech and very little freedom of the press.

Shakur's quest to tell the truth and uphold the basic right to foment change reverberates among all of us. By standing up for her, we take a stand against our government's ominous criminalizing of dissidents and whistle-blowers.

As Shakur's life shows, revolutionaries are not born. They are forged — from historical, economic and social conditions and fighting against oppression. In the United States, founded on 400 years of slavery, Black Americans like Assata are pivotal to building a revolutionary movement.

Dissent and retribution: Justice denied for political prisoners

Mark Cook

))) During my 24 years as a political prisoner, I was transferred more than 17 times to various federal and state penitentiaries. This gave me the opportunity to meet many of the 200 political prisoners who are still incarcerated. Their activism and commitment to changing the politics of the U.S. government have not been altered by their confinement.

I felt honored to share the company of those heroes — Veronza Bowers, Herman Bell, Matulu Shakur, Oscar Lopez, Larry Giddings, Bill Dunne, Adolpho Matos, Jaan Laaman, Leonard Peltier, Fawaz Younis, Jihad Abu-Mumit, Phil Africa, Sundiata Acoli, Anlo Chang, the Virgin Island Five, and so many more. I feel obligated to speak on their behalf whenever I can.

Political prisoners in the U.S. are people whose imprisonment results from actions or beliefs that challenge capitalist politics — the program of those who control our government through campaign funding supplied by the bosses. They are also those social prisoners who become politically active while in prison and get hugely extended sentences as punishment for joining the struggle for poor and working people.

One of the most representative and well-known political prisoners today is Mumia Abu-Jamal. His case raises two critical social and political issues: the political imprisonment of the Left in the United States, and capital punishment.

A fallible legal system, easily manipulated

The death penalty and life behind bars are imposed predominantly on the poor under capitalism. Why? Because those who are impoverished are the most politically volatile faction of the working class. They are unemployed or underemployed and always in the vanguard of economic protests. So it serves the interests of the system to "criminalize" the poor and leftists in order to curb dissent against poverty and discredit organized leadership among the poor.

Canada, like many other nations, rejects capital punishment — not on the grounds that it is a tool of oppression, but because rational law requires an effective process to correct mistakes.

"Legal systems have to live with the possibility of error. The unique feature of capital punishment is that it puts beyond recall the possibility of correction." With these stark words, the Supreme Court of Canada refused to extradite two young Canadians who would face the death penalty in the U.S.

But here in the U.S., Mumia spent 30 years on death row and is now serving a life sentence without possibility of parole. Because he is a revolutionary, he was falsely accused and convicted of killing Philadelphia police officer Daniel Faulkner. The case against Mumia is rife with error — error that conceals his innocence.

Another political prisoner, Leonard Peltier, a former member of the American Indian Movement (AIM), stands convicted of killing an FBI agent on a Lakota reservation. Like Mumia, Leonard seeks release based on evidence not presented at his original trial. Although he does not face the death penalty, his case once again demonstrates the legal system's refusal to face up to its fallibility, because of the capitalist interest in keeping potential organizers of the poor behind bars.

Then we can look at the case of the nine members of the MOVE Organization, a radical Black liberation group. They have been imprisoned for more than 20 years because Philadelphia cops killed a fellow officer and a civilian in a rampaging attack on MOVE's collective house. Why are the MOVE members and not the cops behind bars? Because MOVE articulates the degradation of the system and shows how we can enjoy social justice by exercising community political power.

There are hundreds of cases in the U.S. in which innocent prisoners/defendants have had their convictions reversed because of error or deliberate frame-up. This demonstrates that the legal system cannot be allowed to place these injustices beyond correction with capital punishment.

Prisons as political detention centers

Mumia's trial was held during the early Reagan years of antiradical reaction. Twelve people on a jury found him guilty based on falsified evidence, evidence withheld, the lies of coerced witnesses, the rulings of an infamously pro-police judge, and the poor performance of a sellout public defender.

Even the rules of the current judicial system say that Mumia is innocent until proven guilty beyond a reasonable doubt. And reasonable doubt abounds. Untried evidence, for example, includes a confession by a man named Arnold Beverly, whose recently released affidavit says he was hired by corrupt Philadelphia cops to kill Faulkner, who apparently was a whistle-blower.

Today, tens of thousands of people around the world find Mumia not guilty, based on facts and evidence never revealed to the original 12 jurors. Can the state's 12 jurors have more power than the people's jury?

The trial jury was no more legitimate than a stacked

deck; the evidence they were allowed to consider was full of marked cards.

Mumia should never have been brought to trial and convicted — and given that he was, he should have been freed long ago. He should never have been threatened with death.

Mumia's situation puts the spotlight on political prisoners in the U.S., whose very existence the government denies. A powerful journalist, Mumia has attracted massive, widely based support to his cause. This has infuriated several political administrations since his bogus trial in 1982.

Because Mumia refuses to be silenced, he has been harassed unmercifully by authorities in the government and the criminal justice system. They persist in mounting obstacles to keep the truth from being told and to forestall the evidentiary hearing that would, if justice prevailed, free him.

> U.S. political prisoners are people whose imprisonment results from actions or beliefs that challenge capitalist politics.

These same official persecutors thwart justice in the cases of more than 200 other political prisoners in U.S. penitentiaries. These prisoners are regularly subjected to corrupt trials and massive sentences because they won't abandon their opposition to the status quo.

People who advocate for freedom for political prisoners do so for many differing reasons. This should not, however, dissuade them from moving in common to rein in the intimidation and terror this government imposes on its people through imprisonment. The varying interests of grassroots anti-war groups during the Vietnam conflict did not prevent those organizations from coming together and helping to stop an unjust war. The same show of solidarity is necessary to save Mumia and win freedom for all political prisoners.

Society's obligation to right the wrongs

During the 1950s, the McCarthyism that made anti-establishment politics "un-American" was open and overt. Today's witch-hunting tactics against dissidents are more subtle and refined. But they are just as dangerous to the entire community in the U.S. today as in those bygone days.

Now we face our greatest social obligation: correcting the legal system. To do that, we must replace capitalism with a political system more responsive to the interests of the masses — socialism.

I see politics as the struggle for power over society and the economy. All the political prisoners I have met and talked with agree that the poor and working class must enter into struggle against the corporate bosses, who buy the congressional leaders and legislators who run the country.

Capitalism has no respect for human dignity or human life. It is a barbaric system, and capital punishment and political detention are its barbaric tools. To my sisters and brothers inside, I say stay strong. I salute your sacrifice.

Escalating police violence renews demand for elected civilian review boards

Emily Woo Yamasaki

Police brutality is on the rise and out of control. Cop violence against people of color, immigrants, and the poor is the status quo. Racial profiling — identifying people as criminal suspects based on their skin tone — is a daily reality. Forceful repression is the rule at demonstrations addressing grievances from the economic scorched-earth policies of the World Trade Organization to the frame-up of African American political prisoner Mumia Abu-Jamal.

It's no wonder that people all over the U.S. are taking to the streets and saying *"Basta* — enough!"

National epidemic

As a New York City resident, I cannot forget the 41 cop bullets pumped into Amadou Diallo, the horrifying assault against Abner Louima, the shotgunning of Eleanor Bumpurs, the indifference of officers to the sexual violation of more than 50 women in Central Park, and the trampling of marchers by mounted police during a memorial for Matthew Shepard.

From 1994 - 2000, the Big Apple paid $176.9 million to settle more than 3,500 misconduct lawsuits. And all but one of the cops involved evaded any disciplinary action!

Police abuse is not only a New York "thing." It rages coast to coast, from San Jose, California, where an attack sent Aaron Rivera to the hospital for immediate brain surgery to save his life, to Philadelphia, where videotape captured Thomas Jones being kicked and mauled.

Rooted in inequality and injustice

In a capitalist society, wherever there are police, there will be police brutality — because the cops' main job is to protect big business and private property. It is a given that they will use force to guard the "haves" from the "have-nots" and to repress dissidents.

The link between the class role of the cops and institutionalized racism, moreover, is an old one. The first police unit in colonial America was formed to capture runaway slaves! And, as special targets of the cops, historically and currently, African Americans always have taken on key leadership in fighting back.

In the 1990s, as Bill Clinton continued to shred the social safety net, living conditions deteriorated, provoking more crime and political resistance. In response, authorities launched a proliferation of "law and order" campaigns, including "zero tolerance policing," that give cops a license to terrorize the poor and people of color. This is where today's sharp increase in police violence comes from.

The hypocrisy of the crackdown on crime is appalling. Wife-beaters, gay-bashers, anti-abortion fire-bombers and shooters go unpunished; sheriffs and ICE (Immigration and Customs Enforcement) agents work hand in hand with anti-immigrant vigilantes on the Texas border. Meanwhile, all over the country, young men "guilty" of nothing but dark skin are harassed and persecuted.

Whose streets? Our streets!

During the last two years, the anti-police abuse movement has grown to a new level.

In New York after the Diallo shooting, Black leaders initiated protests that attracted people of all colors, students, teachers, Jews, queers, and immigrants. Weeks of mass civil disobedience, during which more than 1,200 people were arrested for rallying at NYPD headquarters, led to the indictment of the four cops who gunned Diallo down. The subsequent acquittal of the officers ignited a whole new series of demonstrations. Women, too, are on the front lines against police brutality. I was among hundreds of grassroots feminists and women of color who rallied to condemn the cops' role in the Central Park attacks in June 2000.

But even the most murderous cops are rarely censured, let alone convicted in court. We need a concrete mechanism to deal with those who abuse and kill.

Goal: community control of the cops

At a Radical Women meeting in NYC called "Feminists Face Off Against Police Brutality," Juanita Webster of the Black Radical Congress called for authoritative and representative civilian review boards to curb cop outrages. Webster, RW members, and others present discussed the conditions necessary for review boards to be effective.

First, the boards must be made up of people *elected* from the community, not "yes men" or "yes women" appointed by city officials. This is a central demand of longtime organizers against cop atrocities such as former Black Panther Michael Zinzun, head of the Coalition Against Police Abuse in Los Angeles.

Moreover, the boards should be administratively and financially independent of the police and able to conduct investigations and subpoena witnesses, not just review internal police inquiries.

Finally, they must not be merely "advisory bodies" but must have the power to make policy and to fire and discipline cops. And each needs to be complemented by an independent special prosecutor.

Nobody is under the illusion that review boards will *eliminate* cop depredations: these will be a fact of life as long as we have a social and economic system that exploits the majority for the benefit of a few. But widespread boards, representative of the working and poor people who are the favorite targets of the uniformed men in blue and black, could certainly *reduce* police rampages. And they could provide some recourse against cops who now murder and maim unrestrained. These are reforms worth fighting for!

And as part of the battle, anti-abuse activists should call for a presidential Executive Order mandating the creation of elected review boards in *every* city where the viciousness of the cops has shown the need for them.

People of color, immigrants, the homeless, youth, women, queers, dissenters, and striking unionists all have the *legal right* to be free from police abuse. True, that right is violated every hour. But by uniting with each other in the streets and on civilian review boards, we can take some important steps toward making that right on *paper* a right in *reality.*

Georgia prison strike:
A multiracial revolt against
slave-labor practices

Mark Cook

))) *"On Monday morning, when the doors open, close them. Do not go to work. They cannot do anything to us that they haven't already done."* This was the message that inmates got on the fifth day of a strike that became the largest prison strike in U.S. history.

When it began on Thursday, December 9, 2010, strike leaders planned a one-day, peaceful, self-imposed lockdown in several Georgia state prisons. Their headline demand was an end to slave labor in the state, which by its own "law" compels state prisoners to work without pay. Fifty-four thousand inmates, *the largest single workforce in the state,* work for Prison Industries, a subsidiary of the Department of Corrections — and get paid nothing.

The inmates' intentions were 1) to mount a multiracial protest against a southern prison system infamous for violating human rights and practiced at pitting one group against another; 2) to educate the public on the intolerable conditions of life for incarcerated people; 3) to demand recognition by prison authorities that the U.S. is supposed to be a democracy, which minimally means the abolition of slavery and the right of everyone — including ex-cons — to vote and have a voice in improving a rigged justice system.

Their work stoppage was a conscious labor rights offensive that demonstrates growing class-consciousness among the millions of people behind bars in this country.

Sit-down strike, not riot

All of the men were outraged at their slave conditions. They could have rioted. Instead, they organized a sit-down strike and prepared a list of demands. They used contraband cell phones purchased from guards to communicate between prisons. And because of certain retaliation, the identity of strike leaders remains a mystery.

The prisoners didn't get violent. The guards *did*. They pepper-sprayed, handcuffed and beat inmates with hammers, threw many into solitary confinement, turned off heat and light utilities, secretly transferred strike activists to other prisons, offered gang members money to attack other prisoners, and more.

"They want to break up the unity we have here," said one inmate. "We have the Crips and the Bloods, we have the Muslims, we have the head Mexicans, and we have the Aryans all with a peaceful understanding, all on common ground. We all want to be paid for our work, and we all want education in here. There's people in here who can't even read." Black men are 61 percent of the state prison population, whites 36 percent.

What do they want? The public to understand that prisoners are a hidden labor force not counted in the employment statistics. They are workers, not animals and want to be treated fairly as working-class citizens. As a reporter with *Black Agenda Report* put it, "With one in 12 Georgia adults in jail or prison, on parole or probation,...*prisoners are us.*"

Workers halted the strike after the sixth day to counteract the brutal crackdowns on them and, as one said, "So we can go to the law library and start...the paperwork for a lawsuit."

Although the mainstream press largely ignored this historic work stoppage, word got out through the independent press, community activists, prisoners and their families — all

Ex-prisoners participating in a Detroit rally in support of the Georgia prisoners' strike in December 2010.

armed with cell phones.

The Concerned Coalition to Respect Prisoners' Rights formed, and was swamped with messages of solidarity. Meetings and marches took place in Oakland, Detroit, New York and Raleigh. Because of public pressure, seven prison guards were arrested on February 21 for assaulting one of the many inmates beaten.

Similar conditions exist nationwide. Two and a half million adults are not allowed to vote because they are in prison. Five times that number — on parole, community supervision or probation — can't vote and are blocked from employment and education opportunities, healthcare service, special housing, etc.

Basic demands

The Georgia strikers presented the following nine demands, which eloquently testify to the conditions of U.S.

imprisonment and what's needed to help inmates make it once released. The demands form the basis of ongoing negotiations between Georgia officials and the strikers.

A living wage for work: In violation of the 13th Amendment to the Constitution prohibiting slavery and involuntary servitude, the Department of Corrections (DOC) demands prisoners work for free.

Educational opportunities: For the great majority of prisoners, the DOC denies all opportunities for education beyond the GED, despite the benefit to both prisoners and society.

Decent healthcare: In violation of the Eighth Amendment prohibition against cruel and unusual punishments, the DOC denies adequate medical care to prisoners, charges excessive fees for the most minimal care and is responsible for extraordinary pain and suffering.

An end to cruel and unusual punishments: In further violation of the Eighth Amendment, the DOC is responsible for cruel prisoner punishments for minor infractions of rules.

Decent living conditions: Georgia prisoners are confined in over-crowded, substandard conditions, with little heat in winter and oppressive heat in summer.

Nutritional meals: Vegetables and fruit are in short supply in DOC facilities while starches and fatty foods are plentiful.

Vocational and self-improvement opportunities: The DOC has stripped its facilities of all opportunities for skills training, self-improvement and proper exercise.

Access to families: The DOC has disconnected thousands of prisoners from their families by imposing excessive telephone charges and innumerable barriers to visitation.

Just parole decisions: The Parole Board capriciously and regularly denies parole to the majority of prisoners despite evidence of eligibility.

Four decades in prison: Interview with Black Panther leader Eddie Conway

Chris Smith

The Seattle Freedom Socialist Party sponsored a Black History Month forum in 2011 titled "The FBI's War on the Black Panther Party: The Fight is Not Over!" The featured speaker — from behind bars — was Marshall "Eddie" Conway: author, Vietnam vet, and former Panther leader in the Baltimore chapter. Conway was sentenced to life imprisonment in 1972 after being framed for killing a Baltimore cop. His two books are entitled THE GREATEST THREAT and MARSHALL LAW: THE LIFE AND TIMES OF A BALTIMORE BLACK PANTHER.

In April 2014, Eddie Conway was finally released from prison as the result of a ruling by Maryland's highest court that tossed out hundreds of convictions. After 43 years and 11 months, Conway was out and unrepentant. He immediately called for an ongoing struggle to free all political prisoners.

Below are excerpts from Eddie Conway's 2011 phone interview with Seattle FSP organizer Chris Smith.

Smith — *What was it about the politics of the Black Panther Party and your own experience that helped you to decide to join that organization?*

Conway — I think it wasn't so much the politics of the Black Panther Party as it was the lack of progress in any other avenue that we attempted to work through. When I returned home from Europe, from the army, I joined the NAACP and

I joined CORE. Both of these organizations were trying to integrate workplaces, change the laws and improve conditions in the community. Through that process I found out that the problems in America were systemic and so profound that all the reform organizations couldn't really address the conditions of the Black community. A bunch of us decided that we needed to have something a little more solid and tangible and the Black Panther Party represented that.

Smith — *What made the Black Panther Party different from some of those other organizations?*
Conway — Our community was impoverished. And there was a lot of police brutality against our young people, a lot of police "justifiable" homicides occurring. We recognized the need for some sort of organization that would address that and challenge the police, try to get community control of the police. The other organizations weren't even talking about this, or about us setting up an apparatus that would take care of us and use our own resources such as health clinics, etc. The Black Panther Party was talking about these issues, and it was very appealing.

Smith — *Right. Not only were they talking about it, but they were defending the community. What do you see as the role of women in the Black Panther Party?*
Conway — I always feel like women were probably the glue that helped the party grow and develop and manage itself — logistically in terms of making sure the programs operated, in terms of even studying. Women had equal roles in the Black Panther Party. A lot of people talk about that. In fact, I always tell people that when sisters and brothers both are required to know self-defense mechanisms, there's not going to be a lot of male chauvinism or discrimination within an organization.

Smith — *What did you do in the Black Panther Party? And what contributed to your arrest and imprisonment? Tell us your story about how you were set up.*

Conway — In Baltimore I was a lieutenant of security for a period of time, so I was responsible for checking new members. I discovered that the defense captain in the Baltimore chapter was actually a National Security Agency agent or agent provocateur, and that he had been sent to Maryland to set up an artificial Black Panther Party. I became the target of COINTELPRO after that, because my exposure had caused them to lose a key spy, and they put me on their hot list, I guess.

There was this incident in which two members of the Black Panther Party got arrested a couple of blocks away from the scene of a crime, and they engaged in a shooting incident with Baltimore city police. One of the police was killed, one was wounded and one shot at. A day or so later they arrested me and charged me with being the leader of that. When they couldn't substantiate it, they put an informer in my cell who had worked for the police department before, and he turned in the statement they needed for a conviction.

They had no evidence. All the people who testified at my trial were police officials, and one or two work supervisors who testified that I was organizing Black postal labor. I worked for the Post Office then, and I was organizing Black postal workers to create a union for us, because we weren't getting fair representation from the major union.

Smith — *The Panthers called themselves "Revolutionary Internationalists." How did they come to that position and what does it mean?*

Conway — Initially, we were Black community focused — we attracted a lot of Black nationalists and a lot of people who were just really concerned with what was happening in the

Black community. But as we looked at who our friends were and who our enemies were, it became clear that our problem wasn't one of us being a colony or having a nationalistic problem. Our problem was a class struggle, because it was clear that there was something wrong with the way the economic system had been set up and how it impacted a large portion of the Black community. We recognized that the same problem existed in South Africa, in Nicaragua, in Vietnam, in the Middle East, and that we must really look at the situation from an internationalist perspective. Our philosophy elevated to Revolutionary Internationalism.

Smith — *In 1968, FBI Director J. Edgar Hoover called the Black Panther Party the single greatest threat to the security of the U.S. What was Hoover afraid of?*
Conway — The United States military was like five million people and of course they had the most sophisticated weapons on the planet. So you'd think, "Well OK, what's the problem here?" The problem certainly wasn't a military threat! The problem was the possibility of Native Americans, Latinos, the anti-war movement, the New Left and the old Left, the Palestinians and Puerto Ricans, the Africans and Asians and Latin Americans — all these people working together in some sort of unified way.

The idea of them supporting each other really did represent a threat in Hoover's mind. And a threat to the ruling class itself, because for the first time the youth and progressive people were challenging it in the street. And for the first time since McCarthyism, I think there was a clear understanding that people were talking about the "no-no" word, socialism.

Smith — *What advice do you have for young African Americans and other radicals of all colors who want to see change?*

Conway — We need to educate, spread the word, and work on the ground in the areas where we can. We need to network at this point. Because I think that what's happening in Ireland is coming to America, what's happening in France is coming to America, what's happening in Egypt is coming to America, what's happening in the rest of the world — all those things are coming to America.

3. THE BORDER CROSSED US

What drives Latino children to El Norte?

Hugo Orellana

))) Sixty thousand children from Central America walked over the U.S.-Mexican border and, for a few days in 2014, the world looked up from war in the Middle East and the problems between Russians and Ukrainians and paid attention.

These were not just any children. Though some of them were still in Pampers, they had the most unusual powers. As word spread of their arrival, chaos followed. The haters mobilized to send them back to whatever slum they'd come from. President Obama shed crocodile tears while counting up the cost to house and feed them. Lawyers talked about closing legal loopholes big enough for five-year-olds to walk through. Even the usually unflappable, well-dressed presidents of Mexico and Central America rushed to the White House for photo ops, eager to push the children off the nightly news.

While the radio hosts rattled on about the dangers of terrorists on tricycles, many folks acted shocked and surprised that the children had come so far, mostly alone, across such dangerous territory. It seemed the U.S. had a bad case of mass amnesia.

Does the public remember nothing about the civil wars in El Salvador, Guatemala and Nicaragua? Of the dictatorships the U.S. backed? The Honduran coup blessed by Saint Obama? The U.S. invasion of Panama? Don't they have a clue where their 60-cents-a-pound bananas come from and at what cost? Apparently not.

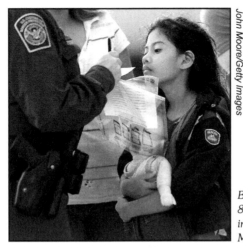

Border Patrol takes an 8-year-old Salvadoran girl into custody at the Texas/Mexico border.

It seemed that 60,000 children had walked out of history and into the U.S. consciousness to remind the Yanquis that Manifest Destiny has intertwined our destinies.

Take the case of Guatemala. In 1954, the CIA orchestrated a coup d'état against President Jacob Árbenz Gúzman because he had begun to distribute land to the hard-pressed peasants. This challenged the rule of United Fruit Company, the largest landowner in Guatemala. A friend of the State Department McCarthyites, its exploitation of the people knew no ethical or legal bounds.

The coup d'état divided the Guatemalan army. Some officers were bought off by the CIA; others helped launch the guerrilla movement, realizing that conditions for indigenous peasants were unbearable. This unleashed a civil war 36 years long in which many died. In 1996, the two sides signed peace accords, but peace was still elusive.

Instead, the accords launched another kind of war. Many of the young and traumatized kids of that time, as well as the young adults with the scars of the war fresh on their skins, fled to the north and found refuge in the romanticism of gang culture in big cities like Los Angeles and Chicago.

Within a decade of being involved in gangs, they were tangled up in the U.S. judicial system and introduced to prison culture. This was followed, sooner or later, by deportation to Guatemala or another Central American country wrecked by war and free trade. Once home they unleashed what they had learned in gang life: extortion (known as "war taxes"), enlisting children for criminal activities, and terrorizing poor neighborhoods. All this in communities where people tried to live decent lives, already punished by wars and the endless parade of corrupt governments.

Then Obama started deporting nearly half a million people a year. Families trying to put lives back together in a foreign land were re-traumatized and divided by ICE raids on buses, in schools and homes, and at traffic stops. Now there were more orphans on both sides of the border.

In Central America, these kids joined others left without family by criminals, poverty or government policy. They set out from their home countries ready to do whatever they had to do to find a better life. They suffered hunger and abuse on their way north. And it wounded their little psyches to be shoved aside like the Dalits (untouchables) of India once here, after they had endured such an odyssey. But regardless, they were undoing Obama's mass deportation policy and putting it on its head.

It turned out there is something stronger than U.S. imperialism. It is the children's hunger for safety, for a roof over their heads and, most of all, for the love of their families. It pushed them across mountains and cities, across deserts and rivers. It's why they took care of each other.

Band-Aids and temporary fixes from NGOs (non-profit service agencies) won't stop this exodus. More children are leaving today to make the journey north and more will leave tomorrow. Until there is justice in our hemisphere, the children will give us no peace.

Border town blues:
Life in Nogales and Juárez

Noel Perez

))) I was born in a small town in Mexico, in the state of Jalisco, and I moved to Los Angeles in 1974. Once a month I visit Nogales, Mexico, a town in northern Mexico on the border of Arizona. My wife is living there while we wait for her visa. She has been there for over two years.

Of the 150,000 residents in Nogales, 50 percent are employed, and 50 percent are jobless or under-employed. The ones that have a job work at factories or *maquiladoras*. If you are lucky and have a good job, you will make 2,000 pesos a week ($168). Most families have one person with a visa, and they go to the U.S. to buy food, because it's 20 percent cheaper.

Most people in Nogales don't have a job that pays $168 a week; half of the population is in other types of work. A lot of people work in the drug trade or the trade of moving people over the border, or taking money as bribes from the drug lords.

I visit my wife once a month. After my first visit, I noticed a weird vibe in the air — people were cold, most would walk from work to home without a smile, without the warmth and kindness I was raised with. I couldn't figure it out.

But it didn't take long for me to find out what everyone was going through in Nogales. A month later, while I was waiting for my wife to get off work, I walked into the store to buy an ice cream. Right behind me, a man ran in. He shot a guy who was sitting there eating, and then he ran out. On the floor was a dead man with his head blown off. I looked and saw everyone running, so I ran.

Ten hours of driving back to LA, and all I could think of was how everyone changed right after the murder. People who live in that border town *know* someone will be murdered, but they don't know who or when. When it happens, pressure is released and it takes a day to build back up — just 12 hours, not months or weeks. But in those few hours Nogales changes. You see smiles. You see life. Nogales police reported 3,000 killings in one year. But at a demonstration against all these murders, they said it was more like 5,000.

> In Juárez, the biggest industry is drugs; the second largest is the U.S. Consulate.

We had to go to Juárez, because it is the only place you can get a visa to come to the United States. Juárez is a big city on the Rio Grande, just across from El Paso, Texas. It has twice the number of factories as Nogales. But the biggest industry is drugs. And second largest is the U.S. Consulate.

Here's what they put people through to get a visa. It took all day to get into the consulate. Then they tell you they will let you know by DHL shipment. They say it takes three days to get the packet. It took me and my wife three weeks. You can't call anyone to see what is happening. You just wait. Then after three weeks, we get a letter saying they need to make a decision and they will get back to us in one year.

I saw a lot of people who did not have money for hotels just walking outside all day and night. Someone is making a lot of money from the hotels and food. Maybe that's why they call the area around the consulate the *zona de oro* — the gold zone.

You need a doctor's exam that costs $150, plus shots. My total bill was $435. You have to be there for three days to get the doctor's results. We went to the consulate. My wife is told, "You can't leave Juárez. You will get a letter by DHL in two to three days." Again, it took three weeks for us to get that letter. I spoke to a lot of people who were told the same thing, but they had been there for two months — waiting.

We were trapped in Juárez. Seventeen kids at a party had been gunned down and the city was on lockdown. No one could get in or out. Drug cartels run the streets, hundreds of women have been murdered going to work at *maquiladoras* and no official seems to care, because they have been corrupted by the drug money flowing through the town. Meanwhile, there are over 3,000 Mexican troops protecting the U.S. Consulate.

If drugs were legal, there would be no drug cartels or corrupt police and public officials. If borders were open, no foreign-owned factories would cluster in these towns paying desperation wages. Juárez and Nogales exist *only* to exploit the workers, and as way-stations to smuggle drugs and weapons.

Here in the U.S. we should fight for an open border, an end to the drug war, and an end to the trade agreements that have wrecked the Mexican economy. Then Mexico could go back to being a beautiful place.

Obama's cruel immigration hoax

Yolanda Alaniz

The sparring between President Obama and Congressional factions about immigration reform covers up a basic fact. Not one plan being floated would create a better life for undocumented workers; each would instead increase the everyday terror these immigrants face.

This is true for a simple reason: top-down immigration reform isn't designed to help immigrants — it's designed to help business.

Obama's game plan

Comprehensive immigration reform proposals generally have three main components: cracking down on what's defined as illegal immigration; offering the hope of legal status for immigrants currently without papers; and enlarging guest worker programs.

Obama's blueprint, put forward in detail in 2011, reads like sci-fi.

At the border, it would increase the fences, drones, agents, cameras, and radar already multiplied by Obama.

It would make mandatory the E-Verify program that employers use to check job applicants' status, which could easily lead to requiring ID cards for everyone. And the plan would introduce a biometric identifier like fingerprinting or a retina scan into hiring.

The misnamed "path to citizenship" is the carrot to attract popular support for Obama's wretched plan. But don't be fooled! The path is strewn with daunting obstacles: "rigorous security checks," a series of fines, competency in English, payment of back taxes.

After all this, undocumented immigrants would still have to wait until the current backlog for green cards (the first step toward citizenship) disappears. Immigrants in some categories could wait 20 years!

When it comes to guest worker programs, Obama is playing it coy. He says he supports agribusiness having the workers it needs, but doesn't spell out what this means. With an eye on staying competitive with capitalists abroad, Obama is definitely in favor of making it easier for highly skilled immigrant STEM workers (science, technology, engineering, math) to stay in the country.

For now, Obama seems to want to let Congress, labor officials, and the Chamber of Commerce slug it out over the guest worker issue. But Obama will do what he must to make sure business can keep maximizing profits — while also trying to keep Latino voters firmly in the Democratic Party camp.

License to exploit

From the large Bracero Program begun during World War II to dangerous cleanup after Hurricane Katrina, guest worker programs typically lure immigrants forced by desperate life-or-death situations to take temporary, low-paid work exempt from normal labor protections.

Tied to one employer, they must keep their job to keep their work visa. Bosses can control them with the threat of deportation if they try to organize a union, demand standard wages and decent conditions, or report abuse or sexual assault. Their super-exploitation lowers pay and conditions for all workers.

Republicans in Congress insist that guest worker programs be part of any reform. The Senate "gang of eight," tasked with developing a bipartisan plan, agrees — with details yet to come.

As Obama pointed out, his plan and the bipartisan committee's have a lot in common. But the gang of eight wants to make the path to citizenship even more of a sham, by requiring proof that the border is "secure" before issuing the first green cards!

Labor-business hookup

In February meetings, AFL-CIO President Richard Trumka and Chamber of Commerce CEO Tom Donohue agreed on three things: U.S. citizens should have the first opportunity for all U.S. jobs; a new visa should be created that allows guest workers to switch jobs and permits some to become permanent workers; and the future immigration of low-skilled workers should be regulated by a new federal bureau based on "market needs."

Trumka reportedly endorsed a new temporary worker program at the meetings. He later said that any final deal involving guest workers must include a path to citizenship and labor protections.

This is a retreat from the AFL-CIO's previous staunch opposition to guest worker schemes and its support for amnesty. Agreeing to any program that makes immigrants second-class workers breaks with "An injury to one is an injury to all." To their shame, several unions, including SEIU, have supported guest worker programs in the past.

It will be to Trumka's shame if he does the same. It doesn't bode well that he is trying to forge an agreement with labor's exploiter, big business, in the first place.

Demand what's really needed!

Our sci-fi novel seems about to take a turn for the worst, where identity chips embedded in people's brains control them, everyone works for The Corporation, and drones stand guard.

But wait! Underdog heroes always rebel before the end.

Here and now, protesters in San Jose, California carry signs saying "No back of the line approach." Gerald Lenoir of the Black Alliance for Just Immigration makes gritty criticisms of Obama's scheme, including his omission of refugees and so-called criminals. Alexandra Suh of the Koreatown Immigrant Workers Alliance asserts, "We must all demand that he stop deportations."

But many major immigrant rights NGOs are missing in action. They have nothing to say about how nearly impossible it will be to become a citizen. No criticism of E-Verify, which will track workers like cattle. No condemnation of abuse of guest workers or the assault on civil liberties through border militarization and prison growth. No scathing words for Obama, who boasts of deporting a record 400,000 immigrants in a single year! Their silence is a way to keep the most exploited and oppressed workers in the Democratic Party. Sellouts!

The U.S. Bracero Program ended in 1964 after decades of laborers being underpaid, overworked, harassed, and poorly housed. The Department of Labor officer in charge of the program called it "legalized slavery."

As a former farmworker who lived in the worst labor camps possible, I say never again!

I look forward to the revival of the militant movement — to once again seeing rank-and-file immigrant women lead a million strong down the streets, demanding what immigrants really need and what the Freedom Socialist Party and Radical Women have always called for: Unconditional and immediate amnesty! Stop the deportations and ICE raids! No Bracero Program! Union wages for all! Give workers the freedom that corporations have — open the borders!

No welcome here:
An immigrant's saga

Hugo Orellana

If you have not been an undocumented immigrant from Central America making your dangerous way through Mexico only to face vigilante hate groups and *la migra* at the U.S. border, you don't know what hell is.

Fleeing poverty or persecution at home, you are exploited and persecuted again by Mexican police trying to rob your last coins. If you're broke, you wind up in a Mexican jail, charged with a fabricated list of crimes from A to Z.

Next you could find yourself being tortured by the *federales,* using techniques like those of the Guatemalan military, who learned them at the School of the Americas at Fort Benning, Georgia.

If by a miracle the planets are aligned in your favor and you get through Mexico with no problems, and if you are lucky to have family willing and able to help you with cash, you still find yourself at the mercy of the "coyotes," the smugglers of humans.

These experiences make the TV program *Survivor* look like a walk in the park. Yet they are just a sprinkle of the storm that awaits you once you make it into the promised land — and they are only the first pages in the book of my own life.

During the 1980s, when I was in my 20s, I spent six months at the Port Isabel immigration processing center in Texas, together with 600 other Central American men and women escaping civil wars and seeking political asylum.

At Port Isabel, we were left outside in heat up to 100 degrees, while dust storms swept through the camp and invaded our bodies. My ears became infected, and it took several days of complaining before anything was done. Even at that, I was fortunate, because I spoke some English; others could not.

During my first few days there, we weren't provided with hygiene necessities like soap and toothpaste. Because there were no portable toilets outside, people had no choice but to just pee on the ground. When the guards saw this through their surveillance cameras, they would shout racist insults.

After 15 days, a prisoner would be called for a hearing, and bail would be set between $15,000 and $35,000. The way we were ripped off by the Mexican *federales* was nothing compared to this. How are poor immigrants supposed to come up with this much money, even if they have employed family members in the U.S.? Many detainees had panic attacks at the thought of being deported back to countries where they would most likely be killed by death squads.

If you have not been an undocumented immigrant from Central America, you don't know what hell is.

Corruption and brutality were widespread. One time, a guard offered me food and money to beat up a detainee he had clashed with a few days earlier. I just walked away.

Another time, a Salvadoran prisoner from my barracks was slow to leave the courtyard when we were called in for lunch. An officer struck him, drawing blood. The detainee wanted to take legal action and talked to people at Proyecto Libertad, an immigrant rights project. At midnight, after the lights were out, about five immigration officers came into our unit, seized the injured man and his witnesses, and transported them to Houston, where they were deported.

This so-called democratic system failed these people. The constitutional rights that they are supposed to have as human beings in this country, regardless of race and national origin, were thrown in the gutter.

In Mexico and Central America, 90 percent of the people live day by day, just trying to make ends meet. Many depend on agriculture to survive, farming their own small piece of land or working for someone else. But they cannot compete with massive tons of cheap agricultural products from the USA, flooding in thanks to "free trade."

This gives people no alternative but to leave. Those who own houses or livestock sell them, others borrow money. A lot lose everything in their trek up north, and the ones who get deported back return to a miserable existence, worse than when they left. What way out is left for these wretched of the earth except revolution?

But, like a curse, U.S. capitalism has been riding right by our side for what seems like forever, with the *Yanqui* government stopping us from pursuing our own destinies by supporting one oligarchy and genocidal military dictatorship after another. Still, don't think for a minute that our spirit of revolution has been shot. Now more than ever, as we see movements in South America making advances toward better societies, we are inspired to struggle.

But the people of Mexico and Central America also look to the native-born citizens of the U.S. to fight to get *Tío Sam* off our backs and to wage your own battles. After all, you have a history of making revolution; perhaps you can make just one more, in the cause of gaining freedom for all of us.

Chaos ensues in film satire when Mexicans in California disappear

Yuisa Gimeno

California without Mexicans?! As unbelievable as that sounds, it's the basis for the comic fantasy *A Day Without a Mexican,* directed by Sergio Arau and co-written by Arau, Yareli Arizmendi, and Sergio Guerrero.

A Day Without a Mexican begins when a mysterious fog surrounds the entire state of California and one by one every Latino goes missing. ("Mexican" in the film includes not only Mexicans but all Latinos from Central and South America as well. The joke is that most white people in the film seem not to know the difference and treat all Latinos the same.)

Chaos unfolds as a senator's family struggles to get breakfast ready and laundry done without Catalina, the domestic worker. A farmer worries about losing his crop without pickers. People ransack grocery stores for the last fruits and vegetables. Some white bigots celebrate the disappearances with a barbecue. Politicians in Sacramento call a state of emergency.

A heroine's quest for her people

The story of the "mockumentary" centers around Lila Rodríguez (played by co-writer Arizmendi), a television reporter who is the only Mexican American to survive the disaster.

To find the solution to bringing her people back, she donates her body to science and, under the watchful eyes of the U.S. military and government, endures grueling experiments.

After learning that there really is no sincere intent to restore her people, Lila escapes from the hospital. Hoping to find answers, she sets out to cross through the fog at the border of the United States and Mexico. She yells, "I must find out where they are and bring them back!" as immigration agents stop her.

After Lila is forcibly returned to the hospital, the viewer learns the reason that Lila did not disappear along with other Chicanos and Latinos — in a surprising and moving twist that will not be revealed here!

Chilling implications

Along with the comedy and plot, the film serves up statistics about California and the one-third of its people who are Latino.

It may not be too hard to imagine what the absence of every Latino would do to agriculture, the state's top industry. But the movie provides other facts that fill in the picture. Gone would be 20 percent of K-12 teachers and 60 percent of construction workers.

Also gone would be the $100 billion that Latinos contribute to the California economy.

In truth, the state would go belly up without the cheap labor of Latinos and their spending as consumers.

Despite this, the economic, political, social and cultural contributions of Latinos are neither valued nor acknowledged. Instead, Latino/a labor is made invisible. Or worse yet, many people at times buy into the stereotypes, seeing Latinos only as criminals who terrorize the streets, or as welfare mothers and "illegal aliens" who mooch off the system.

A Day Without a Mexican ends with the fog miraculously lifting and all the Mexicanos and Latinos beginning to reappear. California's crisis comes to an end and everyone is overjoyed.

This includes even the U.S. Border Patrol agents. The immigration service is portrayed as caring about how Mexicans are treated, an event that would be extremely unlikely outside of the movies.

Reality check

What is happening in actual life?

According to the *Los Angeles Times,* Border Patrol officers in Southern California have been increasingly questioning and arresting Latinos. More than 100 Latinos recently have been arrested while getting off public buses, shopping in grocery stores, or simply resting in their homes.

Racial profiling and roundups of Latinos under the guise of fighting the bogus "war against terrorism" tear families apart. Latinos in California *are* vanishing before our very eyes. The fog of bigotry is indeed very thick in California.

A Day Without a Mexican doesn't pretend to give all the answers. Instead, it uses satire to show how immigrants and Mexicans and all Latinos in the United States are human beings who built, and continue to build, this nation. And it is high time that society learned to value their contributions.

The movie has generated controversy, but as a Latina and an activist, I wasn't offended by its satiric humor. In fact, my stomach hurt at times because I couldn't stop laughing. I appreciated its sharpness in exposing the ironies that in reality wouldn't be so funny: untended leaf blowers spinning out of control, restaurant owners panicking because they have to wash dishes. It shows that if the cheap labor of all immigrants did evaporate one day, businesses would be living a nightmare — especially agribusiness.

So, if you want to see a film with sidesplitting comedy that doesn't insult your intelligence, and in fact challenges it, go spend an afternoon or evening "without a Mexican."

4. SISTERS DOING IT

From graffiti girl
to organizer:
My revolutionary education

Miriam Padilla

*I am from drive-bys, sirens, and the cries of a desper-
ate mother asking for help. From the city of lost souls,
the city of angels. I am from beans, rice, and leftovers
to the endless streets of taco stands. I am from Aztec
dancers. I am from feminism and activism.*

I have witnessed first-hand how poverty and inequality affect the human spirit. As the daughter of immigrant
parents from Mexico who only speak Spanish, I grew up in
poverty in South Central Los Angeles. I grew up watching
my parents struggle to make ends meet. Often, we didn't
have enough money for food, electricity or water. Many
times my dad went out to Home Depot, waiting long hours
for someone to hire him to paint or garden at their homes –
long hours he could have spent with his children. All of this
because of his immigration status.

When my mother crossed the Mexican border carrying
my older sister, who was only seven months old at the time,
she was forced to stay in a home with a dozen other immigrants until someone paid the *coyotes* for her release. My
mom always reminded us that the reason why she came to
the U.S. in the first place was for us to have a better future.
By example she taught my siblings and me to have pride and
pushed us to get an education. It was our key to opportunity.

My adolescent years and poverty, however, blinded me

to this opportunity. When I was 12, I started sneaking out of the house to escape the reality of my everyday life. One night I befriended a group of graffiti artists and eventually graffiti became all that was important to me. I started skipping school and, by the end of my sophomore year, became a high school dropout. Not long after, I learned I was pregnant and decided to move in with the father of my baby, which was a poor decision. I ended up dependent and trapped, with bruised eyes, busted lips and bite marks.

A couple weeks after I gave birth, my mom asked me to move to Seattle with her. It was a new start for me. I met up with other teenage parents and we created a space to support each other and to pursue an education. Then I was lucky enough to be introduced to Ida B. Wells High School for Social Justice, a public school program for youth from tough backgrounds who want to go on to college. Here I was exposed to political activism and taught the truth about oppression: where it comes from and why. It was very liberating. Suddenly one sees the bigger picture. My teachers understood that for us it was not a matter of being limited or incapable of thinking academically, it was more about needing a clear understanding of why things are the way they are.

History teaches us about the forces that create change. And it is from this power that people like us, the working people, can liberate ourselves from oppression. I have gained a greater understanding of the complexities surrounding social inequalities, fueled by what I have experienced and suffered first-hand.

In early 2013, I spoke at a public forum about immigration sponsored by the Freedom Socialist Party. In the following months I worked with the party and became actively involved with many other struggles, such as the fight by berry workers to unionize at Sakuma farms in Burlington, Washington.

During the last couple of months in high school, I flew

back to South Central Los Angeles to help organize the 2014 Freedom Socialist Party convention. Going back home reminded me that because I have the opportunity to reach for higher education, I should not forget my people back home. I must continue to be a motivator, and is my responsibility to make it easier for the next generation to achieve too. Today, my goal is to receive a BA and continue to law school so that I will have the capacity to help others. Although I have faced difficult social challenges, I have not given up and my interest in educational growth and social activism continues.

For the past year and a half I've been part of the campaign to free political prisoner and indigenous leader Nestora Salgado, a naturalized U.S. citizen being held in Mexico. Salgado was unjustly imprisoned for leading an indigenous community police force in the state of Guerrero, but her case has broader implications, from environmental justice to police brutality. Nestora is the face of universal human rights. Reminding us that a revolutionary change is necessary.

Working on the Freedom for Nestora committee has taught me organizing and leadership skills, and how to work collectively. This campaign has empowered me to speak up for myself and others. The first week of my college career I organized a couple students and myself and together we formed a committee to free Nestora in Olympia, Washington.

I want my human rights respected. And together we can achieve this. We must actively voice our interests now. There are so many social injustices facing our society today that cry out for radical solutions and new leadership.

I have learned the courage to take control of my life, and am determined to break boundaries. Through hard work and a strong sense of hope, I look forward to a future where Nestora, my daughter, my community and my class will live free.

Clara Fraser:
Mentor for revolutionary feminists of color

Norma Gallegos

))) I learned about Radical Women at the beginning of the new millennium. I had just left high school and started at City College of San Francisco. I was hungry for revolutionary politics that were feminist and spoke to who I was: Chicana, queer, poor, and a born-and-raised San Francisco city gal.

I was riveted by Radical Women's weaving together of socialism and feminism. Socialism is the theory that liberates women and all oppressed peoples worldwide by destroying capitalism and establishing a planned, sustainable economy. Socialist feminism dismantles patriarchal, racist, sexist, and homophobic institutions. It gives us the power to educate, learn, live, breathe, eat, sleep, work, love and take care of each other.

Many of these ideas are dynamically expressed in documents written by Clara Fraser (1923-1998), a founder and leader of Radical Women and the Freedom Socialist Party. Although I didn't know Clara personally, I have met her through her writings.

Woman as leader

My first introduction to Clara's writings was *Woman as Leader: Double Jeopardy on Account of Sex*. This essay defies what we have been taught by capitalist patriarchal education when it asserts, "In the beginning, in the matriarchate, woman was leader...social and political equality prevailed."

The definition of "leader" in the document is very important. Clara notes:

> I use the term "leadership" in the political, rather than...
> business tycoon sense. A leader leads others, expresses, and
> influences the ideas and feelings of others, and acts in con-
> cert with others to change the social and cultural climate.

Leadership is natural to women. It is inherent in all of us but under capitalism women leaders face hostility. Clara says:

> Women are oppressed as an entire sex...judged to be
> biologically, emotionally, mentally, and temperamentally
> inferior to men. Female ambition was the sign of the devil...
> the acting out of penis envy, and the childish refusal to
> grow up and have the proper kind of orgasm.

For a woman to think and act is an outrage, a freak of nature, and if she's a radical she needs to be reprogrammed immediately. But hey, if she will *échale ganas,* that is, if she will keep on truckin', she will evolve into a radical leader who, as Clara says, "exults in taking on the power structure, and the populace, with a multi-issue, revolutionary double-barreled blast."

The path to freedom

In *Which Road towards Women's Liberation: The Movement as a Radical Vanguard or a Single-Issue Coalition?,* Clara explains that even if we win reforms on single issues, like abortion rights, we wind up fighting to retain them year after year.

> The single-issue is the dead-end issue. It is an inevitable vio-
> lation of revolutionary clarity, integrity, and responsibility,
> yet it persists because the ruling class confers respectability
> upon it.

If women wise up and turn to multi-issue causes and a multi-issue program to win freedom, it becomes a challenge to capitalism. *The logic of multi-issuism leads inexorably to anti-capitalism.*

In *Which Road,* Clara emphasizes two main points:

1. Women's liberation can only be attained by a multi-issue movement of radical women.

> Through *every* mobilization and on *every* issue, radical women steadily work to radicalize the *entire movement* and expand the vanguard itself. Without such leadership, the women's movement, like *every* other movement, will petrify, corrode, adapt and drown inside the Democratic Party or inane single-issue liberalism.

2. The woman question has a dual and triple nature; it is therefore a multi-issue question.

> Working women are exploited as workers and doubly exploited as female workers, since their special oppression as a sex permits extra exploitation of them in their capacity as workers, and for minority women, racial oppression adds a third focus of suffering.

Some women's groups want to play it safe by only seeking reforms. But I joined RW because of its bold anti-capitalist program. We want to take control of the whole system to benefit all of us. Power in the hands of capitalists means total destruction of our planet. Power in the hands of socialist feminists means enabling the entire working class to transform our world and help it flourish.

Women's emancipation

Clara writes in *The Emancipation of Women* that it was no accident that a Black woman worker, Rosa Parks, sparked the Montgomery Bus Boycott and inaugurated a new era in

American politics.

> ...as a worker, a Black person, and a woman, she represent-
> ed the three strands of American repressive culture; every
> prejudice focused on her and she felt deeply the threefold
> nature of the fight for freedom. She was destined objec-
> tively for her function today as the vanguard of political
> consciousness, spirit and vitality; in Mississippi she runs for
> Congress, organizes farm labor unions and schools, con-
> fronts and confounds the Black men of her own movement
> with her initiative and firm resistance to all their attempts to
> subordinate and subdue her.

The leadership accomplishments of Black women and
women of color are massive in the face of racism and sexism
and the oppression of workers. Ambitious, yes! Hungry, yes!
Hell-raisers, hell yes!

I'm a daughter of Mexican immigrants and grew up
with a lot of people of color around me. At one time, I was
confused about who had it better or worse — immigrants
or Blacks? But now I realize that it is not a ranking of oppression that matters but who leads to unite us for radical
change. Women of color are triply oppressed — quadruply
oppressed if we are queer. This doesn't mean we get to "play
victim" harder, it means we need to fight harder to be leaders. We go to the mat for everything we are.

Clara Fraser and the origins of the Comrades of Color Caucus

Radical Women and Freedom Socialist Party members
of color are also part of the Comrades of Color Caucus.
This caucus was formed on the initiative of Clara, a Jewish
comrade, to elevate the "people of color question" so that
all members of RW and the FSP would prioritize the fight
against racism. The CCC was formed in the '80s when some

disgruntled white members (who were in the process of abandoning radical politics) claimed that RW's stand on the leadership of the most oppressed actually tokenized women of color members. In response, RW members of color defended the program and at Clara's suggestion formed the CCC in collaboration with men of color in the Freedom Socialist Party.

The caucus helped me see that I can work with white members who are anti-racist activists on my side of the class line. My sisters of color in RW have shown me how we can confront and stop incidents of internal racism and taught me that I can stick to my principles in a multiracial organization without letting go of my Chicanisma.

The CCC serves as a leadership body that analyzes the issues of race and racism to educate our members and fight together against it. Clara was at the helm in showing comrades how to confront racism and anti-Semitism with a fighting socialist feminist program with leaders from all walks of life.

As socialist feminists we make change for the whole working class, by the class, with class and a lot of sass! Socialist feminist politics have been tested and will be the vanguard in the war against capitalism. We are on the right side of history and our legacy proves it. *¡Adelante!*

40 years after *Roe v. Wade:*
Women of color lead fight for reproductive justice

Nancy Reiko Kato

))) January 22, 2013 marked the 40th anniversary of *Roe v. Wade*, the U.S. Supreme Court decision legalizing abortion in 1973. The court based its ruling on the idea that for government to outlaw abortion would violate a woman's constitutional right to privacy.

This was a historic triumph for women's rights, won by the influence of a cresting feminist movement. Still, it was always a limited victory. The court said that while states could not ban abortion, they could restrict it — giving the right wing an opening that they have taken ferocious advantage of.

And, as important as the right to abortion is, it is only one aspect of reproductive justice — especially for women of color. Reproductive rights mean the right to free, safe abortion on demand; access to safe birth control; no forced sterilization; accurate, inclusive sex education in the schools; and social support like childcare, workplace leave, and well-paying jobs for parents, including lesbian, gay, bisexual, and transgendered parents.

Women of color in the U.S. have always resisted laws and practices denying them reproductive choice. Because they are more likely to be poor — over 23 percent of women who are Black, Latina, or Native American live below the poverty line — and because they experience racism as well as sexism, their stake in being able to control their own bodies is magnified. These facts also make women of color the strongest defenders of all aspects of biological self-determination.

Early fighters for reproductive choice

In the days of slavery, African American women, whose children would be born into bondage, sometimes covertly used traditional methods to prevent and end pregnancies, which were often the product of rape. In the early 1900s, Black women in Harlem were active in the movement for birth control.

And, in the 1970s, a lawsuit and grassroots organizing by Chicanas in Los Angeles were key to ending, in most of the U.S., an official policy of forced sterilization of women deemed racially, mentally, or physically "inferior." As an internee in the U.S. concentration camps for Japanese Americans during World War II, my own mother narrowly escaped this fate when a proposal in Congress to sterilize women of Japanese heritage in the camps failed by *just one vote.*

The campaign to legalize abortion in Washington State is an excellent example of militant, multiracial organizing, one that resulted in success three years before *Roe v. Wade.* Black women from anti-poverty programs joined with Radical Women members to form Abortion Action Now. They linked the need for abortion to an end to forced sterilization, demanded affirmative action and free 24-hour childcare, and recognized that without justice on the job and in the home, there is no equality.

These ideas resonated with working women and men who marched, rallied, and spoke at public hearings. The pressure forced legislators to put legalized abortion to a public vote; it passed decisively.

Continuing to take the lead post-*Roe*

The right wing has never given up its crusade to eradicate the right to abortion.

When *Roe* first went into effect, poor women could use

federal Medicaid funds to cover the cost of terminating a pregnancy. But this ended quickly when the Hyde Amendment, which denies Medicaid funding for abortion, took effect in 1977.

This ban caused the death of Rosie Jiménez, a young Latina mother who was six months away from her college graduation when she was refused funding for an abortion in Texas. She turned to a back-alley butcher and died from septic shock in October 1977.

For women of color, the stake in being able to control their own bodies is magnified by poverty and racism.

Every year, thousands of poor women are forced either to have a child they cannot support, driving them deeper into poverty, or to risk their lives with unsafe terminations. And every year, politicians from both sides of the aisle reaffirm the Hyde Amendment.

Meanwhile, reactionaries use every means imaginable to make abortion unobtainable, from legal restrictions to fire-bombings of clinics and assassinations of doctors. Eighty-five percent of U.S. counties now do not have an abortion provider.

In March 2006, after South Dakota's legislators passed an abortion ban, Oglala Sioux President Cecilia Fire Thunder announced that she would defy the ban and open a Planned Parenthood clinic on tribal land. She paid for her courage with impeachment by the tribal council. But her bold leadership was a pivotal schooling in how to fight back and helped set the stage for a massive voter rejection of the ban later that year.

Also in 2006, in July, Operation Save America (formerly Operation Rescue) announced they were going to Mississippi to shut down the state's last abortion provider, the

Nancy Reiko Kato calls out a chant at the 2009 mobilization against the annual anti-abortion "Walk for Life" in San Francisco.

Jackson Women's Health Organization.

Michelle Colon, an African American social justice activist, put out a call to come to Mississippi to defend the clinic. The response she got included young Black women, lesbians, students, and Radical Women. The reproductive justice troops, who outnumbered the anti-choicers, went door to door to gather support, held rallies and a press conference, and sent the misogynists packing. However, the state governor continues to maneuver to close the clinic.

In 2010, 65 billboards equating abortion with genocide suddenly sprang up in Atlanta. They showed a tearful Black child next to the words "endangered species."

Outraged by this attack on Black women, SisterSong, a national group of women of color for reproductive justice, worked with others to found the Trust Black Women coalition. The coalition organized a successful campaign to educate about the dangers of racialized anti-abortion tactics, and their leadership inspired protests in other states where the billboards appeared.

Forging ahead

Reproductive justice activists of color must contend not only with the right wing, patriarchal politicians, and sexism in their communities and society broadly. They must also deal with leaders of the mainstream feminist movement who are often unwilling to fight for the reproductive issues that most affect women of color, like forced sterilization, unsafe contraceptives, and denial of public services to undocumented immigrants.

These more conservative feminists also rely, in vain, on Democratic Party politicians to protect women's rights.

For feminists, the anniversary of *Roe v. Wade* is not a time for self-congratulation. It is a time to take to heart the lessons of the struggle for reproductive justice and renew the fight.

As Michelle Colon says, "The war is in the streets, and folks who don't have anything are the best activists. We must incorporate all women into the movement or else we will lose."

Let's celebrate *Roe v. Wade* by getting back to movement-building.

"Comfort women" of WWII: From sex slaves to human rights warriors

Merle Woo

))) Japan's "comfort women" system — the official and extensive enslavement of young women by the imperial government for sexual exploitation — stands out as one of the most egregious examples of how women suffer the cruelest blows of war. To this day, the Japanese government denies its responsibility for this World War II-era atrocity.

The responsibility is not Japan's alone, however. The U.S. turned a blind eye, as did the Japanese-occupied Asian countries from which the comfort women came.

Then, after a half century of silence, an amazing thing happened. Former comfort women stepped from obscurity and went public with their stories.

Since 1992, survivors living in South Korea have protested at the Japanese Embassy in Seoul. Their goal is to obtain an official apology, with the hope of preventing this kind of crime against humanity from ever being repeated.

But, as elderly survivors die, time is running out. Support for their endeavor by feminists and human rights activists is now more crucial than ever.

Unimaginable exploitation made real

In the first decades of last century, Japan was a huge expansionist force competing with U.S. and European colonialism in East Asia and the Pacific Islands. The comfort women came from countries Japan invaded — 80 percent of them from Korea, which Japan occupied from 1905 to 1945.

Most of the comfort women, who numbered up to 200,000, were poor. Some were girls as young as 10. Representatives of the Japanese government pressed them into sexual servitude with lies, including promises of education, or simply by snatching them from the streets. Usually taken from their home countries to military brothels elsewhere, they were kept isolated and imprisoned.

Enduring serial rapes at night, the women were often also used as worker-slaves and forced to accompany the soldiers in battle.

Grandmother Kim Hak Soon, born in Manchuria and sold by her stepfather to the Japanese military at the age of 16, stepped forward as the first public witness to these horrific abuses in 1991, 60 years after they began. This is what she said:

> During the daytime, we delivered ammunitions, cooked, did laundry and worked as nurses. During the nighttime, we were forced to serve Japanese soldiers. If we rejected to do it, even a little, we were beaten...or pulled in hair and dragged naked. ...We were never paid. We never saw a penny.

More than half of the women died while enslaved. Some were tortured to death. Some became ill and were denied medical care. Others died of starvation or from involuntary abortions and sterilizations.

After Japan lost the war, the women were murdered or just abandoned. Many traveled for years to get to their home country, or never returned.

Others besides the comfort women also suffered inhuman exploitation sanctioned by the super-militaristic Japanese government. Japan conscripted huge numbers of forced laborers, probably millions of them, to work in mines and other Japanese industries throughout the region. These were men from Korea, China, and other occupied areas, plus Allied prisoners of war. And more than 100,000 people died as a result of Japanese biochemical warfare experiments.

A wide circle of complicity

One of the stated reasons for the comfort women system was to maintain the "purity of Japanese women." However, when the Allies occupied Japan in August 1945, the imperial government immediately established comfort stations for *them,* using poor Japanese women. The stated reasons were to protect "respectable" women, prevent a rampant spread of venereal disease, and placate the occupiers in order to avoid uncontrolled rape and pillage.

Crimes against women, historical or occurring today, are not taken seriously by those in power.

Nevertheless, even after the end of the war following the bombings of Hiroshima and Nagasaki, U.S. soldiers occupying Japan raped, extorted, and murdered with impunity. They called the comfort women "communal toilets" or "yellow stools."

There is ample, concrete evidence for official Japanese responsibility for the system. Still, the former Allied powers and the victims' countries of origin have never prosecuted Japan for this war crime, although organizing by and on behalf of the comfort women has stirred some of them to criticism.

Racism is a key reason for this, since most of the women were of color. Even more basic is that all of the countries involved are members of the same capitalist club, despite the brutality with which they have ravaged each other during two world wars.

Specifically, following WWII, the primary interest of the United States was to rebuild Japan into a strong economic power to help in the Cold War fight against communism. Even as late as 2001, Washington, D.C. actively opposed a class-action lawsuit filed in the U.S. by former comfort women demanding redress from Japan.

Capitalism relies on patriarchal values. Contempt of women is the norm. Crimes against them — like the social and sexual crimes occurring today against Iraqi women, and against female U.S. soldiers fighting in Iraq — are not taken seriously by those who hold power.

Moving forward

The surviving comfort women want to change that. For years, they have picketed in front of the Japanese Embassy in Seoul every Wednesday. As their numbers fall, they have continued to demand a formal apology from Japan plus compensation.

In March 2007, after it had become fairly commonly accepted even in Japan that their sexual coercion was official policy, Prime Minister Shinzo Abe publicly and flatly denied it. Nationalistic school textbooks approved by the Ministry of Education omit all information related to this and other wartime atrocities by Japan.

Although some measure of justice is yet to be won, the comfort women have increased consciousness and given impetus to raising the status of wartime rapes to an internationally recognized war crime.

Diverse groups around the world have held public hearings, tribunals, and conferences and passed resolutions in support of the comfort women. Ongoing solidarity is needed to support the protests in Seoul and efforts to include the truth in Japan's textbooks.

Even more important is that feminist and human rights activists fight to end imperialist wars! Men who become soldiers are not naturally the enemies of women brutalized during war. The blame belongs to the social and economic system whose profits depend on both war and women's subjugation.

Grandma Kim Hak Soon died in December 1997. In an interview with Dai Sil Kim-Gibson, an advocate for comfort women, she said, "I want the Japanese to give us a signed document in which they acknowledge that Japanese colonialism was wrong...a crime, no matter how you look at it — legally, politically or simply humanly."

Hidden from history:
Bennett College women and
the Greensboro sit-ins

John Hatchett

The author calls this piece "necessary reminiscences" con-
cerning an event that is often credited with launching the civil
rights movement of the 1960s: a sit-in campaign by African
American college students to integrate the whites-only lunch
counter at a Woolworth store in Greensboro, North Carolina.
When the young people were denied service on the first day
of the sit-in, February 1, 1960, they refused to leave, and the
lunch counter was shut down.

Over the next two weeks, as the Greensboro students contin-
ued to sit in, similar actions spread to 15 Southern cities.

More than 50,000 students participated in the new move-
ment that year, and 3,600 were jailed. By the end of 1960,
many lunch counters across the South — including the one at
the Greensboro Woolworth — were segregated no longer.

))) The story I want to share with you is designed to correct a long-standing inequity and remind us that we
shall know the truth, and, hopefully, the truth will set
us free. I dedicate this proposition to a fundamental
conviction that as a people we African Americans are as
victimized and dehumanized by untruth as we are by racism.
   On February 1, 1960, four young Black men from A&T
College of North Carolina sat at Woolworth lunch counter
in Greensboro and requested service. Thus was born the

modern-day sit-in movement.

But what led up to that moment in time, and what really triggered the decision made by the four young men? This is the untold story — hidden, ignored, distorted, falsified, and denied by the media.

Young college women with social conscience and commitment

In September 1959, I came to Bennett College, a historically Black women's college also located in Greensboro, to teach philosophy and religion and social science. The college chapter of the NAACP (National Association for the Advancement of Colored People) asked me to be their adviser. I readily consented.

I came from a family environment where social activism was encouraged. My parents taught me that telling the truth was more the measure of a real man and woman than anything else in life. They further taught me to respect and like myself and to do likewise unto others but never to allow anyone to run over me.

I had come to Bennett College from Alabama A&M College in Normal, Alabama, where I served as the Acting College Chaplain and taught courses in history and sociology from 1958 to 1959.

During my brief stay at A&M College, I was instrumental in helping the student body mount a successful campus boycott against the repressive social and intellectual atmosphere which prevailed on this campus.

As a result of the students' discipline and determination, some substantive changes were implemented which benefited the entire A&M campus. It was this background which I brought to Bennett College.

The members of the NAACP campus chapter were young women of intelligence with a social conscience and an unusually high degree of commitment. They were unequivocally opposed to racial injustice and desirous of changing the racist status quo that prevailed in Greensboro. They wanted informed guidance and fearless leadership and felt that I met their strict requirements.

Woolworth chosen as target of desegregation

From September until early November, we met constantly and discussed viable strategies to implement our goals — the first being the desegregation of all places of public accommodation.

We sought information regarding tactics from the youth chapter of the NAACP in Oklahoma City. They had already engaged in an effective sit-in demonstration that led to the opening up of certain restaurants in that Southwestern city.

As a result of our intensive and sometimes provocative discussions, coupled with the data from the Oklahoma City youth chapter and my insights based on similar tactics successfully pursued in my native Pontiac, Michigan, we agreed on our first target. It would be Woolworth's lunch counter.

Our decision was rooted in a tactical and practical reality. Woolworth was a national chain heavily patronized by Black people all over the country. We had anticipated the real possibility of a boycott locally and nationally. We knew we would need all the sympathy and support we could get.

Just prior to the Thanksgiving recess, we shared our plans with Willa B. Player, the president of Bennett College. She displayed no opposition whatsoever but offered us some sage advice which would necessitate a change in our strategy.

She reminded us of the status of the college. It was essentially residential. Most of the students were neither native to Greensboro nor to North Carolina. The long Christmas recess was only a little over a month away.

If we inaugurated the sit-in, who would sustain the

momentum until we returned?

It was a perspective which cooled our passionate ardor, but the sobering reality could not be denied.

I have said that these young women were intelligent, resourceful, and committed. With the support and blessing of Dr. Player, we decided to include the students from A&T College in our discussions, especially the male students. On this score, the charming and attractive ladies from Bennett College had no problems whatsoever.

> The young women of the Bennett College NAACP were unequivocally opposed to racial injustice.

In a series of nightly meetings Monday through Friday and sometimes on the weekends, we met, discussed, debated, refined, and finalized our strategy.

It was agreed that sometime between the Christmas recess and the return of the Bennett women to the college the students from A&T would put our idea into execution, and we would support them upon our return. Included in the contingent of students from A&T were all four of the young men who were destined to become the "Famous Four." They heard; they participated; they believed; and they accepted.

Setting the record straight

What occurred on February 1, 1960 was not the result of a casual dormitory conversation on the campus of A&T College. February 1, 1960 was the culminating point of an idea rigorously thought through, meticulously researched, and enthusiastically debated and refined by a handful of courageous young Black women on the campus of an all-women's college where learning and social activism were inextricably intertwined and endorsed.

It is not a matter of credit. It is a matter of fairness, justice, and truth.

In the women of Bennett College and their adviser and teacher, the word and the deed coalesced and became one. Not only did we have the idea, but we also sustained the sit-ins once they started.

This is the reality. Perhaps, one day, the men from A&T College will come forth and corroborate the deeds of their sisters, thereby ennobling the dimension of Blackness, authenticating the quest for truth, and bringing us closer together as a people of decency and dignity in this Brave New World of Orwellian madness. Truth is really more enduring than fiction, and a million times more precious.

Profile of Black women movers and shakers is revelatory but flawed

Merle Woo

))) Fabulous history fills *Want to Start a Revolution? Radical Women in the Black Freedom Struggle* (New York University Press), edited by Dayo F. Gore, Jeanne Theoharis, and Komozi Woodard. Profiled are indomitable, courageous Black women leaders of the 1930s through the 1970s who provided the organizing backbone in many movements simultaneously: Black, feminist, anti-colonial, pan-African, and socialist.

These are stories of Black women who lived lives of militant activism and then taught the young. Vicki Garvin and Shirley Graham Du Bois, who in this book comes out of the shadow of her husband, W.E.B. Du Bois, mentored Malcolm X. They, along with Esther Cooper Jackson, were communists, labor leaders, feminists, and internationalists long before second-wave feminism and Black Power hit the scene in the '60s.

Esther Jackson's theory that Black women's location at the bottom of the economic ladder positions them as the vanguard for radical change, and that Black women's freedom can only be achieved by the destruction of all forms of domination, was the inspiration for the Combahee River Collective and the Third World Women's Alliance. These groups believed that multi-issuism leads logically to anti-capitalism.

The anthology also covers Toni Cade Bambara, Rosa Parks, Shirley Chisholm, Flo Kennedy, Assata Shakur, Johnnie Tillmon, Denise Oliver and Yuri Kochiyama. Although

Black men were the recognized leaders and often repressed the leadership of women, these women's unquenchable dedication lifted everyone as they rose.

The issues they dealt with remain relevant today. The question of Black women's right to reproductive choice is still key as the U.S. government dumps Norplant and Depo-Provera on Third World women and denies funding for abortions — while some Black cultural nationalists still insist that abortion is genocide.

On the positive side, it's eye-opening to learn or be reminded that organizations like the Black Panther Party and the Puerto Rican-centered Young Lords Party were not exclusive to one race. Japanese American Yuri Kochiyama was an important educator in Malcolm X's Organization of Afro-American Unity. And African American Denise Oliver was a political pacesetter in the Young Lords.

Want to Start a Revolution? offers numerous resources for follow-up, and the footnotes after each author's contribution are a treasure trove of information and historical research sites.

But the book also has its disappointments. It gives no sense of how activists today can use these biographies. Most of the contributors are academics, and the book's disconnect between the struggles of yesterday and today reflects an established trend in Ethnic Studies and Women Studies. Racism and sexism and homophobia are put into the bin of history. All these ugly realities are apparently irrelevant in the "post-racial society."

How can we build a mass movement to win the fundamental change that eluded these woman warriors of the past? To give us tools to choose the right path, our radical education must include analysis and evaluation — which this anthology neglects.

The book's title refers to "radical" women without differentiating between reformists and revolutionaries. In talking about the Left, the book focuses mainly on the Communist Party (CPUSA), Maoism, and revolutionary nationalism. This mishmashing of terms and groups without explanation is confusing at times, perhaps purposefully so.

There is no criticism of the CPUSA as it followed the political zigzags of the Stalinized USSR, which included dropping the fight against U.S. racism during WWII. And there is no mention of the Trotskyist Socialist Workers Party, with its thousands of Black members during the period discussed. This amounts to a historical cover-up.

Finally, it is appalling that a book published in 2009 doesn't give credit to the Black lesbian, gay, bisexual, and transgender movement and its leaders for theorizing a Black revolutionary feminist program. Pat Parker was ignored completely. Audre Lorde is referred to primarily as a poet. And the Combahee River Collective is mentioned briefly, without saying they were Black lesbian feminists — who explicitly stated the need for a socialist revolution that is feminist and anti-racist.

This omission is all the more unfortunate because of the many militant queers who, due to their rock-bottom social status, devoted their lives to the movements the book discusses but could not be "out" at the time.

Despite these serious flaws, *Want to Start a Revolution?* is an important contribution to the history of Black women who built movements. It proves they were the vanguard of the Black freedom struggle, and it brings to light a heroism that is inspiring for those who continue that struggle and others today.

5. SPEAKING FROM THE HEART

When things fall apart: The fate of displaced Africans

Sarah Scott

))) *We Need New Names,* by NoViolet Bulawayo (Back Bay Books), is much more than a coming of age story. It's a tale of savage colonialism, of local tyrants and unremitting droughts and rains, of the shattering pain of having to leave because all things are falling apart. It's the story of one girl's unique trajectory that shares common roads with all immigrants from all places.

Things fall apart

The novel opens in Africa, in the shantytown of Paradise, Zimbabwe. Complex and original characters inhabit its tiny, mud-colored shacks: Chipo, 11 and pregnant by her grandfather — the event that provokes her muteness; Bastard, a boy whose superficial meanness masks his loss of hope; Mother of Bones, who clings to a suitcase of useless old money. These are the family and friends of Darling, the 10-year-old narrator who takes readers on a guava-stealing adventure to ease her starving belly.

Bulawayo's novel is peppered with beautiful similes like "Paradise is all tin and stretches out in the sun like a wet sheepskin nailed on the ground to dry." Each town contains a different world of race and class. Next door to impoverished Paradise is Budapest, a community of better-off whites and Blacks with big houses, where "even the air itself is empty." Next is the industrial town the author names Shanghai, full of terrible machines run by Chinese industrial colonizers.

Throughout their exploits, Darling and friends attempt to

give Chipo a coat-hanger abortion, witness the kidnapping of a white Zimbabwean family by a machete-toting Black nationalist gang, and cope with the return of Darling's long-lost father who has full-blown AIDS. Meanwhile, Darling impatiently awaits the life-saving plane ticket to "Destroyed-michigan," Detroit, where her Aunt Fostalina lives.

Bulawayo offers a scathing critique of foreigners' knee-jerk racism. In greeting an NGO team handing out toys and candy, the kids must be polite to three smiling, white Americans. The visitors' feet have barely touched the ground when they whip out cameras for photos. All adult residents receive a paltry bag of beans and rice, for which they must appear ever so grateful.

Sometimes Bulawayo's writing dissolves into stream-of-consciousness interludes of powerful poetic repetition: "Look at them leaving in droves, the children of the land, just look at them leaving in droves. Those with nothing are crossing borders. Those with strength are crossing borders. Those with ambitions are crossing borders."

Unfulfilled dreams

The book suddenly shifts to the United States. When Darling arrives in Detroit, she sees relatives dealing with forced assimilation in multiple ways. Aunt Fostalina is obsessed with dieting; Uncle Kojo takes long, aimless drives, desperately afraid his soldier son will perish in Afghanistan.

The strength of this section is the author's connections between all immigrants: "The others spoke languages we did not know, worshipped different gods, ate what we would not dare touch. But like us, they had left their homelands behind." Bulawayo eloquently captures the paradox of alienation and sympathy that workers from different countries feel in their common goal to learn English, comparing their reluctant tongues to "staggering drunkards." She writes about the dictatorial immigration service, maids with scalding irons, and tobacco-picking with a hard realism that lends voice to many universal aspects of immigrants' lives.

As Darling willfully detaches from her past and present, these empathic insights dim. She ridicules her friend Kristal for speaking Ebonics, insensitive to chronic racism against American Blacks. Protagonists should not be flawless in novels, but author Bulawayo missed an opportunity to distance herself from the youthful Darling and portray Kristal beyond the stereotypes.

Same goes for Kate, the suicidal, anorexic daughter of a wealthy white scumbag for whom Darling cleans house. Darling considers Kate less afflicted than herself because Kate knows nothing about "real" hunger, trivializing a life-threatening eating disorder and mental illness.

Several years later, Darling's Zimbabwean friend Chipo gets through in a startling Skype call. This, after Darling has ignored Chipo's phone calls for years. Chipo accuses Darling of abandoning her country, family and friends. Although Darling's life choices are understandable, I found myself agreeing with Chipo. It's the first and only criticism of Darling's self-absorption.

The abrupt last scene was troubling. A dog that "chooses" to leave home is eventually killed on the road by a big truck. This may contain great metaphoric potential but it's a sorrowful and misplaced substitute for Darling's slow transformation into adulthood.

Bulawayo seems to believe the harsh journey of immigrants is merely from empty plates to empty lives. A dismal conclusion, however extraordinary her descriptive language.

Luscious poems by Nellie Wong on love, family, revolution

Chris Faatz

Years ago, I worked in an independent Washington, D.C. bookstore. I was the buyer of small press and poetry titles, and I loved it. Week after week, new stuff would come in, and I would be reading political theory and stories and poetry from every imaginable perspective.

One day, I ran across a book with the scintillating title of *Illegal Assembly* by a woman named Karen Brodine. I was relatively new to socialist politics at that time, and a quick flip through it intrigued me, so I brought it home. What I found there was illuminating. For the first time, I discovered that it was possible to meld the ideal of total human liberation with a breathtaking artistic aesthetic. I read Pablo Neruda and Audre Lorde and Roque Dalton. I searched even further, and discovered the Freedom Socialist Party, and through it Karen Brodine's revolutionary socialist feminist sister, Nellie Wong.

Now that was a find worth talking about.

I quickly dug up Wong's earlier books, most notably *The Death of Long Steam Lady*. Once again, the pages of a book of poems opened to a transformative and democratic vista of a brave new socialist world.

Wong's bio, according to the books I read, was short: she was a socialist feminist of color, active in the FSP and its sister organization, Radical Women. Wong had spent a long life struggling both for the immediate rights of the oppressed, and to project the ideal of a world of real freedom, a world where women and men of all sexual identifications and orientations could live and work together as fully realized human beings.

Now, through the good works of San Francisco's Meridien PressWorks, we have a provocative new book by Wong.

Breakfast Lunch Dinner holds, in some ways, no surprises: the poems are deep, fiery, and written from the heart. In the main, they advance, once again, a program for the socialist feminist liberation of the planet.

However, as compelling as the overtly political poems are, this book breaks some compelling new ground as well.

Wong's always written from a number of perspectives. She's written as oppressed woman of color, as socialist, as worker, and as someone who comes from a particular ethnic tradition. In this book, her personal experience of growing up in Oakland's Chinatown plays a much stronger role than it has in previous books.

We read of her family's restaurant (the Great China Restaurant), and how, every day, "precisely at 3:30 P.M.," her mother stops her from reading the paper, and sets her to work typing the next day's menu. It's almost enough to make you think the book belongs in the cooking section of your local bookshop; it's definitely enough to make you hungry!

> My mouth waters
> as she decided the next day's specials.
> Ma doesn't need to say
> Breaded veal cutlets
> Fried oysters or
> Prime rib of beef
> because these were always
> on the menu every day.

Another restaurant, the Sincere Café, offered "the best pork chops/that graced a plate."

There are snapshots of family members (such as Ah Chew Yen Gung — "Stinky Cigarette Uncle" — who's consistently late to work), scenes from the restaurant, from Wong's education as a typist, and her visit to China.

And then, while you get more wonderful food in the last section of *Breakfast Lunch Dinner* (I was particularly smitten with "Ode to Rice Crust Soup"), it also returns both to family and, at last, to some of the most powerful political poems I believe she's written.

As Nellie writes:

> The jingoism dressed in fatigues
> our boys and girls fighting
> over there, in Afghanistan,
> for our sanctity of life,
> for democracy, that old goat
> who used to point his fingers
> at you and off we'd go
> into the wild blue yonder
> killing people who looked like
> some of us in Vietnam,
> in Grenada, in Korea, whatever land
> our government warrants
> needs defending 'cause
> Whoa! Democracy's cool.

One thing that has to be said about Nellie Wong: when she has her finger on the pulse of our world, she is strong and visionary and a literary catalyst for continual struggle. Again and again in poems like "Broad Shoulders" and "I March" and "The Building Song," she rises to the highest ranks of a revolutionary feminist, humanist vision, crafting something that may, at last, after centuries of struggle, give us a reason to battle on.

Asian Pacific America:
Tales from the barricades

Nancy Reiko Kato

))) I'm a homegrown San Francisco Bay Area gal, and I've always felt that revolutionary ideas are in my blood. As a Japanese American growing up in California, I was influenced by the Third World student strikes, Black Panther Party, and Free Speech Movement of the '60s and '70s. But only after reading *Legacy to Liberation: Politics and Culture of Revolutionary Asian Pacific America* (AK Press), have I realized just how much the militant Asian Pacific American (APA) movement helped to shape my Marxist feminist soul.

A groundbreaking anthology representing a diverse spectrum of radical opinion, *Legacy* documents for the first time the rich history of the APA Left, as assessed by its pioneers. The collection, edited by Fred Ho with Carolyn Antonio, Diane Fujino, and Steve Yip, also contains essays, poetry, and art by today's generation of revolutionists.

Radicals paved the path

In his introduction, Ho describes the birth of the APA Left, inspired by Black Power, Vietnamese freedom fighters, and the Chinese Revolution.

Groups formed to provide community services and agitate for sweeping change. Among them were I Wor Kuen, which arose in New York City in 1969; the Red Guard Party, which originated in San Francisco in 1969; and Wei Min She, which coalesced in the Bay Area in 1971. APA barricade-stormers campaigned for Asian American Studies, organized Asian Student Unions, and fought for low-income housing, affirmative action, and tenants' rights.

In the midst of all this, they studied and discussed politics. Their beliefs diverged sharply, but they agreed on the need for an anti-capitalist movement.

Ho urges today's APA activists to revive the tradition of debating theory. "Ideology," he argues refreshingly, "is key to having a framework to advancing strategy and vision and to answer complex questions."

One of the burning questions that APA rebels faced, and still confront today, is whether class exploitation or race oppression is more fundamental. Many of the writers in *Legacy* hold the idea that the fight for race liberation is primary.

This is a position that I and others who work with Radical Women and the Freedom Socialist Party call cultural nationalism. We believe that addressing race liberation is vital — but it can't be at the expense of dealing with issues of sex and sexuality, or of understanding how class divisions underlie all the "isms."

Steve Yip, founder of Wei Min She, is a *Legacy* contributor critical of nationalism. Because it "doesn't challenge the economic relations of capitalist society," he says, "it can't fully represent the interests of the exploited...[and] provide truly liberating solutions to some of the most pressing...problems in our communities — like how to end the oppression of women!"

Or, as Nellie Wong puts it, in summing up a political fight within a Chinese American collective: "Being Asian American alone does not guarantee freedom from conflict."

Changing times, changing movement

After the fervor of the first years, captured in interviews with leaders such as Yuri Kochiyama and I Wor Kuen founder Alex Hing, the revolutionary APA movement receded.

Many groups became more conservative or dissolved.

This was due, *Legacy* essayists note, to the overall social climate of the late 1970s and the 1980s. I think that nationalism also played a significant role: it prevented many leftists from orienting to, impacting, and learning from the feminist and lesbian/gay movements.

Of course these movements, too, have been affected by the changed climate. In "Losing its Soul?" Daniel Tsang points out that leaders of both the APA and gay movements "have become accommodationists with the establishment." Diane Fujino and Kye Leung also offer insight into today's APA movement. They note that many APA organizations are radical, but not revolutionary. The feminist group ASIAN!, for example, decided not to stand for socialism because, its members believed, "few students are ready to join a socialist group."

But Fujino and Leung believe the movement is in an upswing, and they hope that activists now emerging will experience an insurrectionary awakening.

Truly a legacy to learn from

The APA struggle needs both its seasoned veterans and its fresh generations — a political point that is made personally in this volume by the inclusion of pieces by both Merle Woo and her daughter, Emily Woo Yamasaki.

The struggle also needs books like *Legacy*. This anthology is more than just an important history, and more, even, than a foundation for continuing discussions among APA radicals — which are already happening at *Legacy* book readings. In fact, *Legacy* is a model for the type of principled, open, nonsectarian interaction that the different parts of the Left need to have with each other not just between the covers of a book, but in *every* arena of organizing.

For all of that, thanks and thumbs up to Fred Ho and his collaborators.

Bless Me, Ultima:
A Chicano boy's profound coming of age

Yolanda Alaniz

The movie *Bless Me, Ultima* is based on a novel by Rudolfo Anaya published in 1972. Anaya is one of the founders of contemporary Chicano literature, and his book is on many school reading lists, especially for Chicano Studies. It is the first novel shedding a light on the Chicano experience to make it into the mainstream. It broke new ground not only in content but also stylistically, notably in its use of *español* as well as *inglés*.

Carl Franklin directed the beautiful film version. The story takes place in New Mexico during and right after World War II, when many Mexican American youth returned to their *barrios* only to find little economic opportunity after serving their country.

Antonio "Tony" Márez (played by Luke Ganalon) is about to turn seven as the story begins. He experiences the deaths of people around him, comes under the influence of a *curandera,* a healer, and begins to question the beliefs of the Catholic Church. Despite the book's popularity, these themes have made it the target of challenges resulting in its removal from some schools and libraries.

Un corazón dividido

Tony is deeply torn between the influences of his mother's family and his father's. His mother is a Luna (Spanish for moon), and the Lunas are quiet people, settled farmers who have learned to respect the land for the food it provides. His father is a Márez (*"mar"* is sea), a family of loud, wild *vaqueros*, or cowboys, who tend animals on horseback, riding the "ocean" of the plains, always on the move.

His mother wants him to be a priest and his father wants him to be a man of the open range. Tony wants to learn to make his own decisions.

> A beautiful film version of the first novel on the Chicano experience to make it into the mainstream.

Tony attends catechism classes to prepare for his first Communion. He is certain that once he receives the body of Christ he will have answers about death, evil, and where souls go who are not Catholic. After his Communion, he waits with burning anticipation for the answers to fill him up, but nothing happens — and he is very disappointed.

A third influence enters Tony's life when Ultima (Miriam Colon) comes to stay with his family. A *curandera,* she becomes Tony's mentor and teaches him to thank the spirit of the plants and herbs she harvests for medicine.

Growing pains

Ultima asks for Tony's help to cure his uncle, who is dying from a spell cast by three witches. Ultima drives out the evil spirit. Tony does not understand why Ultima can stop evil, but God cannot. And when Tony is exposed to death, he does not understand why God would let a good man die, and an evil man live.

The movie would have been stronger if it had directly shown the emotional connection between father and son. Instead it is adult Tony as the narrator (voice of Alfred Molina) who tells the audience about their conversations. Tony's father explains to him that going through life is what gives you an understanding of why there is evil and why a *curandera* has special powers.

This explanation gives Tony the idea that he can create his own religion — an integration of spiritual folkways, Catholic beliefs, and his family heritage.

Looking for an answer for good and evil

When I was about Tony's age, I also had many questions about Catholicism. I wondered why we were asked to give money to the Catholic Church when we were so poor and why the girls couldn't wear pants like the boys. I was angry at the priest who told my mother she was not allowed to get a divorce from an abusive husband who had abandoned his children.

Later in life, as a product of the Chicano *movimiento,* combined with a spice of feminism and socialism, I stopped attending church. But one Sunday when I was visiting my mother, she asked me to attend Mass with her. The sermon instructed women to stay home and not work; it reminded them that abortion is forbidden and women must obey their husbands.

After the service, I asked my mother if she really believed what the priest said and told her I could not attend church again. She said she did not blame me and would stop attending herself.

The movie is worth seeing and if you missed it, read the book. It reminded me of the role of the *curandera,* respected in our community as a spiritual healer. It brings up the million-dollar question: Why is there evil, and are people born this way? Perhaps taking a scientific, Marxist approach to life, death, and evil within an economic context can lead to realistic answers.

Otherwise, go to church and wait.

Langston lives!
The art of a Black, gay radical poet of the people

Nellie Wong

> Good morning, Revolution:
> You're the very best friend
> I ever had.
> We gonna pal around together from now on.

))) Langston Hughes — the poet of Black people, the poet of all working people, a shining star of the Harlem Renaissance as a writer of poems, prose, journalism, and drama — penned these words during the Great Depression in 1934, the year I was born.

As another radical writer of color, I rejoice at the race and class consciousness Hughes showed throughout his life, particularly in his works of social protest from the 1930s to the 1950s. It warms my heart to rediscover the often buried core of his life and work — the revolutionary man behind the image on the postage stamp.

Blacks creating America

Born in 1902, Hughes grew up poor in the Midwest, shunted between his mother and grandmother and working after school, starting at the age of 12, at a variety of low-paying jobs.

But by the time he was 18, he had already decided to make his living with a typewriter. He cared about his people on the streets, and listened attentively to the music and stories of ordinary African Americans.

In remarks he made upon accepting the 45th Spingarn Medal of the NAACP on June 26, 1960, Langston beautifully captured the profound way in which the contributions of African American artists define U.S. culture, and even world culture:

Robert W. Kelley/Getty Images

There is so much richness in Negro humor, so much beauty in black dreams, so much dignity in our struggle, and so much universality in our problems, in us — in each living human being of color — that I do not understand the tendency today that some American Negro artists have of seeking to run away from themselves, of running away from us, of being afraid to sing our own

Langston Hughes on the stoop of his home in Harlem in June 1958.

songs, paint our pictures, write about ourselves — when it is our music that has given America its greatest music, our humor that has enriched its entertainment media for the past 100 years, our rhythm that has guided its dancing feet....

Our spirituals are sung and loved in the great concert halls of the whole world.... Those of our writers who have most concerned themselves with our very special problems are translated and read around the world.... So I would say to young Negro writers, do not be afraid of yourselves. You are the world.

A door not opened

No one, however, no matter how talented or visionary, completely escapes the constraints of their times.

Throughout his life, to the time of his death in 1967, Hughes was extremely guarded about his sexuality. But what evidence there is makes it clear that he was gay, and queer writers of today passionately number him among their ranks.

Criticizing Langston's estate for refusing to allow his writings to be part of the gay film *Looking for Langston,* poet Essex Hemphill said: "The silence surrounding black gay and lesbian lives is being meticulously dismantled.... Every closet is coming down — none are sacred...those closets are ancestral burial sites that we rightfully claim and exhume."

Seeing through an international lens

Hughes traveled widely, visiting the Soviet Union, China, Africa, and Cuba, and covering the Spanish Civil War for a Black newspaper. The warm reception he received abroad as a Black American writer opened his eyes more widely to the social causes of the suffering of his people in the U.S.

Langston was impressed with the USSR. He reported on the advances made there by Jews, national minorities, and women. While recognizing that the Soviet Union was "not a paradise on earth," he believed that "America can learn some good things" from Soviet progress in areas including race relations and democratic education.

In 1941 Langston published a poem, "Gangsters," still eerily relevant today, that illustrates his sharp sense of class divisions:

> The gangsters of the world
> Are riding high.
> It's not the underworld
> Of which I speak.

They leave that loot to smaller fry.
Why should they great Capone's
Fallen headpiece seek
When stolen crowns
Sit easier on the head —
Or Ethiopia's band of gold
For higher prices
On the market can be sold —
Or Iraq oil —
Than any vice or bootleg crown of old?
The gangsters of the world ride high —
But not small fry.

Langston's positive coverage of the USSR and criticism of oppression and exploitation inevitably drew the attention of Senator Joseph McCarthy, who ordered him in 1953 to appear at hearings investigating "subversion" in Washington, D.C. Under constant pressure to safeguard his precarious economic livelihood, and already having retreated somewhat from his earlier radicalism, Hughes cooperated with McCarthy's committee — but not to the extent of naming names of Communist Party members.

"We have tomorrow bright before us"

Today, whether their medium is jazz, rhythm and blues, rap, hip hop, or the written or spoken word, younger writers and musicians have Langston to thank for the multicultural art that is possible and still flowering in the U.S.

Langston Hughes is everybody's ancestor. He knew that America was big and rich enough to provide for every human being. Through his powerful body of work, through his times of silences and openness, and whether applauded or spurned, Langston lives.

Heart of the Son:
Exploration of the Philippine revolution for independence

Annaliza Torres

))) As a Pinay, a Filipina/o American, I first learned about the fervor of my ancestors in their passionate struggle against the world powers through *Heart of the Son*. This musical drama illuminates the Philippine liberation movement against Spanish colonizers and, later, the United States.

The story raises issues of leadership, and it inspired me to further explore the divisions within the Philippines independence struggle of the late 1800s, and why the movement ultimately failed.

Sining KilUSAn, an all-Filipina/o theater company based in Seattle, put together the performance. They integrate music, dance, acting, and visual arts, considering themselves part of a Filipino American Arts Movement. Directed and produced by Timeteo Cordova, *Heart of the Son* moves the audience by stimulating the senses.

Before the curtain rises, a beautiful piece by guitarist Angelo Pizarro transforms the mood, taking the audience back to when Spain ruled Las Islas de las Filipinas, from 1570 to 1896.

The show opens with a piece called "Freedom Chant." Free of Western influence, it blends percussion sounds from the Philippines, Indonesia, and Africa.

Soon dancers enter, moving to unique choreography created by Bengie Santos, who combines traditional Philippine dance with *arnis* and *escrima*, closely related Filipino martial arts that utilize sticks as weapons.

The story begins in the late 1800s, with a scene that portrays the building of a mass struggle towards independence from Spain. Cordova draws the audience into examining the dynamics of this movement through its two main characters, Andrés Bonifacio and Emilio Aguinaldo.

Which class will lead?

Andrés Bonifacio, a poor worker, founded Katipunan, a revolutionary organization fighting for independence from Spain. As the play unfolds, it shows Bonifacio clearly representing the interests of the working class and leading Katipunan's first armed battle against Spain.

One of the Katipunan's skilled generals is Emilio Aguinaldo, an educated former politician with an elite background.

While the performance shows two separate factions formed around these two men, it doesn't clearly explain the political conflict. This motivated me to better understand the forces behind the contending leaders, and I learned that the division was caused by class differences.

Bonifacio was more grassroots and believed that revolutionary transformation was the only way to ensure independence. Aguinaldo represented more the interests of landlords and capitalists, the *illustrados*.

Eventually, Aguinaldo came to dominate the revolutionary independence struggle that had been initiated by the workers. When Bonifacio denounced Aguinaldo and refused to bow to his will, he was convicted of treason and shot by firing squad in 1897.

Deals among thieves

As for Aguinaldo, I learned that he ended up being used first by Spain and then by the United States to achieve their imperial designs.

Spain bribed Aguinaldo to go into exile. Shortly thereafter, the U.S. declared war on Spain, even as the Philippine independence struggle continued. With Spain eventually severely weakened, mostly from the domestic insurgency, U.S. diplomats convinced Aguinaldo to return and again lead the Filipino people.

Heart of the Son galvanized me to learn the lessons of history in order to more successfully transform our world today.

Aguinaldo declared independence soon after his return, expecting U.S. support. Instead, the U.S. secretly negotiated purchase of the Philippines from Spain for $20 million. In 1898 it declared its domination over the country.

The people continued their heroic fight for independence for another three years in the Philippine-American War. Aguinaldo was finally captured, ending the official war in 1901.

Heart of the Son ends with a stunning monologue by Aguinaldo predicting a future where the U.S. never leaves. His predictions have come true with continued occupation of the Philippines through military bases, financial institutions, political control, and repression of resistance movements.

Heart empowers activists of all colors

Cordova describes the theater piece as an educational and political tool to inspire the fight against oppression. I later also learned how the U.S. used racist and condescending propaganda at home in order to justify its use of money and resources to crush Filipino resistance. U.S. domination of the Philippines enables it to control natural resources like fertile land, coal, and gold, and has helped it access China as a vast market for U.S. products.

The American campaign portrayed in the play marked the early days of the U.S. as an imperialist aggressor on the world scene — a power it could only attain due to its earlier genocide against indigenous people in North America and the enslavement of Africans and their American-born descendants. By the end of the 1900s, the U.S. had colonized not only the Philippines, but also Cuba, Puerto Rico, and Guam as well.

U.S. history began and continues with violence and malice against the world's workers, farmers and peasants, and poor as a way to secure trade and commerce. This experience of U.S. colonization and imperialism, and the accompanying resistance, is shared by peoples internationally.

As long as capitalism promotes the drive for wealth and control of resources, the plunder of other countries will continue. *Heart of the Son* reaffirmed my conviction that a mere exchange of presidents or governments will not change the brutal living conditions for working and oppressed people. The current economic system must be overthrown and replaced with socialism.

For me, the goal of a revolutionary movement is clear: it must keep its militancy and be true to its class. The heart and strength of the masses will not fail when it is workers who lead. *Heart of the Son* taught me to be critical of U.S. involvement in liberation struggles, and it galvanized me to learn the lessons of history in order to more successfully transform our world today.

6. A Global Lens

Make justice prevail:
One Guatemalan woman's
exile saga

Maya Gonzalez

))) I am an undocumented worker. I was trained as an
accountant, a high school teacher and a psychologist,
but that is another lifetime now.

In 1995, I left my house and two children in Guatemala and came to the United States on a visitor's visa with
my youngest child; my husband followed in a few days.

We had been radicalized in the '70s by the poverty of
Guatemala and a series of U.S.-supported military dictatorships. While working as a teacher, my husband was kidnapped twice by the armed forces and tortured. In 1979,
he joined ORPA (Revolutionary Organization of the People
in Arms) and we worked side-by-side in Guatemala City in
support of the guerrilla movement. When my children were
older, I too joined the group.

ORPA was careful to limit comrades' knowledge of who
was in the organization to one other person, so that if you
were tortured you could only give up one name. Still when
the government's counterinsurgency campaign began, the
death squads killed us off slowly, one-by-one. Friends, neighbors and family evaporated into thin air. My brother disap-
peared in the '80s. By chance, a friend of my father's saw
him in a military prison and because my father was a colonel
he was able to save his life.

One month before my father died, someone tried to run
down my daughter and me. We narrowly escaped and I knew

it was a message: without my father's protection, I and my children would be killed.

I arrived in the States in shock. Within three months, a second brother was assassinated at work. There was no investigation. He simply joined 200,000 other men, women and children killed in a U.S.-funded war against "communism."

We immigrant women were victims; now we are warriors, fighting for all the poor and oppressed.

I could have applied for asylum back then, but this required that I remain in the U.S. until I'd qualified. Sounds simple, but I was terrified that the children I left behind might need me in the meantime and I would be stuck here. So I did nothing when my visa ran out.

I started to look for any job I could find, mostly cleaning houses and nursing children and the sick and elderly. For two years, I worked for a newspaper. Sometimes I taught Spanish. I refused to use fake Social Security documents because I believed I had the right to work, an *inalienable human right*.

Fourteen years went by before I began to enjoy my life because the past held me in its grip. The war, the deaths, splitting up my family between two countries — it seemed all I had were memories and nightmares. I tried to block them out, but I couldn't. My mind was in Guatemala for I still dreaded what might happen to my children who as adults became human rights activists.

Simultaneously, anti-immigrant fever spread across the U.S., feeding my old anxieties. When my ex-husband and his new wife applied for citizenship, Immigration and Customs Enforcement told him they were going to investigate his marriage to me. This threat pushed me into a paranoid state.

Because of the history of my country, I dread being sent back as a criminal, with my hands and feet bound.

At times I wonder what will become of me, living between two countries. After a lifetime of work, I have no retirement income in either, and returning to Guatemala is impossible anyway. Femicide is rampant and economically and politically the country is sliding backward. In November 2011, former General Otto Pérez Molina, a past member of the murderous intelligence service, was elected president.

My story is not mine alone. There are millions of hardworking immigrant women in the U.S. who every day face the loneliness, discrimination, violence and exploitation of being women of color workers without the protection of the law. Forced from our own countries by circumstances beyond our control, we are hounded by the Obama administration's immigration police. But we are not blind.

We see that the poor people of this country are as bad off as we are and that everything is getting worse. Like other low-paid women, immigrant women are in the struggle and resisting, conscious that we must be part of bringing to birth a new day by creating unity among all workers, regardless of race or nationality.

Nowadays I sometimes go to the local Occupy encampment and listen to the speeches. It makes me happy because I feel it is the beginning of a big change, part of which must be holding the U.S. government and corporations accountable to the Guatemalan people for the decades-long injury they have done to us, our children and our children's children. We immigrant women were victims; but now we are warriors, fighting — not just for ourselves — but for all poor and oppressed people. We demand vindication!

Solidarity from a Palestinian leader tortured in a U.S. jail

Farouk Abdel-Muhti

Farouk Abdel-Muhti was a Palestinian exile and activist based in New York City. He was arrested several months after the 9/11 bombings and held in immigration detention without criminal charges for nearly two years. The following is an excerpt from his support message for imprisoned people's attorney Lynne Stewart (see page 170). New York FSP and RW worked for Farouk's release in close collaboration with his companion Sharin Chiorazzo. Tragically, Abdel-Muhti died at age 57, three months after being freed from prison.

Is it a crime for a person to talk about human rights, justice and civil rights today? Can it be possible that a lawyer who represents a victim can be accused of aiding and abetting terrorism? Something is wrong here. We need to raise our voices loudly in unity, for justice to come to the rescue of Lynne Stewart. The real terrorists are the accusers and not the accused.

I was incarcerated for almost two years, in nine jails in the United States, enduring physical and psychological torture. Hundreds, before and also after 9/11, have been tortured in these same prisons in the U.S., under the orders of the INS, now ICE, under the direction of the Department of Homeland Security.

It is not necessary to go to the prisons of Abu Ghraib in Iraq, or Afghanistan, or Guantanamo Bay, Cuba to witness torture, because it can be found right here, where U.S. prisons are holding immigrants and detainees, especially those from the countries of the southern hemisphere — Arabs, South Asians and Muslims — for indefinite periods of time, without rights, without charges, without access to lawyers, oftentimes without even a hearing and the basic elements of due process; deporting them in secret when they can, leaving them to languish indefinitely when they cannot. This action destroys families emotionally, financially, and psychologically, and is very damaging to the fabric of this country, which was built and maintained by immigrants.

During my incarceration, I was beaten and degraded, locked up in solitary confinement for more than eight months and 10 days, for 23 hours and 15 minutes daily, with just 45 minutes to make collect calls, shower and clean my iron box. I was provoked every two days by guards, who called me a terrorist, and searched my cell for weapons. Finally, I told them, the only weapon I have is my mind. They cut the water when I was taking a shower, shone flashlights in my eyes and kept bright lights in my face 24 hours a day. They threatened me, mocked and degraded my culture, and put chains on my hands and feet whenever I had visitors, visits from my lawyers, or visits to the clinic. All this, even though I was never charged with a crime and never saw a judge until my habeas corpus hearing, almost two years after my incarceration.

At this hearing, my lawyer argued successfully that I was being held unjustly and illegally because as a stateless Palestinian I could not be deported. I finally won my release, according to the law, and according to the fact that this fair judge saw that what the administration was doing to me was immoral, illegal, and unconstitutional, just as they are doing to Lynne Stewart, and to many others.

This is not just a struggle for detainees, but also against police brutality, racism, injustice, occupation, exploitation and colonialism, denying the working class, marginalized people and others who support the truth, and democratic principles of equality, rights and justice.

Dear brothers and sisters and comrades, I won my freedom through the help of all of you, but we must work hard to win justice for Lynne Stewart and to continue this struggle on the side of workers, immigrants, detainees and all oppressed people who are victims of this imperialistic, lawless machinery that is attempting to hijack our rights.

I also do not forget my native family, and people, the Palestinian people, in the historical land of Palestine, who are waging a resistance struggle of national liberation for their land and rights, for their independence in their own sovereign state, with Jerusalem as its capital and the right of return of our refugees to their lands, homes and properties.

We must not forget to raise our voices in opposition to paying taxes that support the illegal occupation of Palestinian lands, and that support the illegal Israeli war machine, which is using logistical and military hardware supplied by the United States. These tax dollars also send American sons and daughters to die in strange lands, to engage in oil wars for real estate, multinational corporations, and mega-banks, whether in Iraq, Afghanistan, or anywhere else in the world where the United States wants to further its hegemonic and imperialistic designs.

We must cut the tentacles of this demonic imperialism. We can use our unity as a weapon against these designs, without the differences of race, ethnicity or religion coming between us, because we are all one family, fighting in the name of justice, equality and rights. But we must always do this with a view to the principle of the struggle of the working class and marginal people, and those in support of us.

With revolutionary fervor and with great respect, I dedicate this *risala* (statement) to all of you in the name of justice.

The anti-Muhammad cartoons: Behind religious controversy lies class warfare

Statement by the National Comrades of Color Caucus

))) The entire Muslim world was outraged at the publication of several racist, anti-Muslim cartoons in the right-wing Danish newspaper *Jyllands-Posten* in September 2005, and their subsequent publication in other European and U.S. media. Thousands of Muslims in Europe, Asia, Africa and the Middle East hit the streets, protesting, demonstrating, setting Danish embassies afire and destroying Western businesses.

The editor of the anti-immigrant *J-P* claimed he only wanted to "test" the censorship of Islamic fundamentalism, which prohibits depictions of Muhammad. This is hypocritical rot. The cartoons are overtly racist, insulting, and inflammatory. One, for example, depicts Muhammad wearing a turban shaped like a bomb with a lit fuse, neatly dovetailing with President George W. Bush's equation of Islam with terrorism, which he is using to justify the bombing and plunder of Iraq and Afghanistan.

The cartoons promote scapegoating

Media like *Jyllands-Posten* want us to believe they published these outrageous cartoons in order to protect "free speech" against Islamic fundamentalism. In reality, *J-P's* caricatures are a thinly disguised effort to divide and conquer the working class by promoting the scapegoating of Muslims.

To dehumanize, to make different, to make unassimilable

and forever foreign, to turn a targeted group into the other — this is *racism,* and it justifies a group's heightened exploitation by the bosses. Racist stereotypes also isolate people of color by creating distrust and hatred among fellow workers who buy into them.

J-P's cartoons serve a two-fold purpose: they justify anti-immigrant moves in Europe, and they legitimize Bush's "war on terror," including his escalating aggression against Iran and Syria. In the process, religious divisions and oppression are being used to mask class divisions and exploitation.

Governments and racist groups throughout Europe are whipping up hysteria and hatred against immigrants from the Middle East and North Africa — just as U.S. policy-makers and bigots have done for so long against Latinos and Asians. These newcomers, the majority of whom are poor, ill-fed, dark-skinned and struggling to survive, have become a convenient scapegoat for the economic ills of capitalism: runaway unemployment, housing shortages, declining healthcare.

French protest of anti-Muslim racism and ban on headscarves in 2011. The sign reads: "The veil in front of your eyes is much more dangerous than the veil on my hair."

And because the overwhelming majority of these Arab and North African immigrants are Muslim, the campaign against them has taken on a highly religious coloration. A member of parliament with Denmark's second largest political party, the Danish People's Party, has called Islam a plague, comparing it to Nazism.

Especially in Denmark, France and Germany, xenophobic legislation is targeting Muslim immigrants. France, for example, has greatly curbed immigration and banned the traditional Muslim *hijab* (head scarf) from public schools. As journalist Matthew Schofield described it, politicians on the right claim that "Muslims will tear apart the fabric of all that's European." In Denmark, a new law openly aimed against Islamic clerics now bans foreign missionaries from the country.

The scapegoating of Muslims also serves the foreign policy of the United States. The Bush administration has painted all Muslims as possible terrorists to justify the military occupation of Iraq and Afghanistan. The demonization of Muslims is supposed to anesthetize U.S. workers to the crimes perpetrated by U.S. troops.

The mass Muslim reaction against the *J-P* cartoons is ignited by much more than religious persecution, although that is real enough. It is fueled by rage against the imperialist arrogance, exploitation, and military might of European and U.S. ruling elites.

Nationalist governments play on divisions

For their part, regimes in the Middle East tried to cynically manipulate the religious pride and nationalist sentiment stirred up by the cartoons as a diversion from discontent with their rule, and, in some cases, their cozy relations with the United States.

At first, nationalist governments in the region tolerated or even helped to foment the huge rallies against the caricatures. The autocratic Syrian government is widely believed to have been responsible for protests that resulted in the burning of the Danish and Norwegian embassies in Damascus. And Syrian agents reportedly bused in protesters to help swell the numbers in Lebanon.

But when demonstrations turned against domestic ruling classes and the U.S., they were violently repressed and several deaths resulted.

Governments seizing the opportunity to turn attention away from their own crimes also resorted to anti-Semitism. In the Islamic Republic of Iran, Tehran's largest newspaper announced an international competition for Holocaust cartoons as retaliation against the Danish caricatures. Iran was simultaneously in the middle of a crackdown against bus drivers and other workers trying to unionize and organize for better conditions.

Regimes like these would like nothing better than that the conflict over the cartoons be seen as a religious one. Whether secular or religious, they profit from religious fundamentalism, because fundamentalism — Islamic, Christian, or Jewish — ignores class and promotes nationalism as a unifying tool. At base conservative, pro-capitalist, and anti-woman, fundamentalism better enables the owning classes to abuse their workers with impunity.

We are all one working class

Both the "Western" and Islamic ruling classes strive to conquer the working class by using racism, sexism, chauvinism of all kinds, and religious sectarianism. They pit fundamentalist workers against secularists; Christians against Muslims; Muslims against Jews; native-born against foreign-born; white against dark; and long-established people of color against new immigrants of color. A fractured, nationalist working class cannot effectively fight or defend itself against a unified, global capitalist class.

The Comrades of Color Caucus of Radical Women and the Freedom Socialist Party protests the anti-Muslim cartoons because they are an ugly weapon of division among workers.

We call on the U.S. Congress to condemn George W. Bush for equating Islam with terrorism as a rationale for wars for profit and global control. Today, in Iraq, invasion, war and occupation have created poverty, massive unemployment and intolerable living conditions — and the threat of civil war between two Muslim denominations in this once secular country. We join protesters around the world in calling for an end to U.S. and Israeli occupations in the Middle East, and we stand ready to continue to fully defend U.S. war resisters.

We call on the labor movement and the Left to speak out against the racist oppression these cartoons promote and to organize for education, jobs, quality housing, religious freedom, full civil liberties, and the complete benefits of citizenship for all immigrant workers and their families in the U.S. and Europe. It is crucial for unionists, radicals and progressives to educate about the material basis of this explosive "religious" conflict, which at bottom is about increasing the exploitation of the world's working peoples and natural resources.

Let's stand together to say no to racist and chauvinist provocations and schemes and yes to international class solidarity among workers of all religions and colors!

Israeli-born scholar Raya Fidel discusses war hysteria and peace activism

Tamara Turner

Raya Fidel, born and raised in Israel, is a retired professor of Information Science at the University of Washington. She was interviewed by Tamara Turner in August 2014.

Turner — *What is the situation in Gaza?*
Fidel — It is gut-wrenching. The UN calls the level of destruction in Gaza "without precedent." The Israeli military calls the carnage "mowing the lawn."

The latest Israeli military onslaught began on July 8, attacking Gaza from the air, sea, and land. It's easier to imagine the scope if you compare Gaza to familiar places: the entire Gaza Strip of 1.8 million people is the size of Detroit. Gaza City itself is densely populated but small — the size of Napa, the town in California's wine country.

By mid-August, whole neighborhoods in Gaza City — including more than 12,000 homes — were erased from the face of the earth. Despite repeated notices to the Israeli military of where schools, hospitals, and shelters were located, these sites were bombed anyway.

The staggering human toll is now over 2,200 dead (80 percent civilians, including 700 women and children); 10,000 wounded; over 520,000 displaced. Nearly 1.5 million people are without water, food, or electricity. The UN Relief Works Agency is trying to provide for over a quarter-million people — about half of whom are children under the age of

18. An estimated 400,000 children are severely traumatized. Since Gaza's only power station was destroyed, sanitation and disease are a growing problem because most electric sewage pumps aren't working.

Israel's repeated, indiscriminate and unjust collective punishment measures violate international law. Many international humanitarian organizations and hundreds of thousands of demonstrators worldwide accuse Israel of war crimes.

Turner — *How have Israelis reacted to this war?*
Fidel — My friends tell me that most Israelis are in a state of war hysteria — encouraged and abetted by intense government incitement for revenge. Today, 85 percent of Israelis support the war. After three Israeli settlement teens hitchhiking in the West Bank were kidnapped and murdered, a group of Israeli Jews abducted a Palestinian teenager and burned him alive. Protests erupted, and Hamas authorized firing rockets at major cities such as Tel Aviv and Jerusalem. Israelis feared for their lives, though the U.S.-supplied "Iron Dome" missile defense is highly efficient. The civilian death toll in Israel is five.

Inside Israel, right-wing mobs attack Israeli Palestinians — who are citizens! — and there have been several lynching attempts. Calls of "Death to Arabs" and "Death to leftists" are heard everywhere. Goons attack people who "look Arab" and throw rocks at their cars. Palestinian shops are vandalized, and social media channels are filled with extreme hate messages. Police do nothing to protect those under attack and have arrested few of the hooligans.

Another shocking aspect of the hysteria is the rapid deterioration of democracy. Israel as a country is not fascist but it is extremely racist, and the corrosion of human rights goes deep. In general, it's dangerous to express even the slightest sympathy with the Palestinian situation or to criticize Israeli policy. Groups search Facebook sites for "extreme" expressions and report them to the account owner's workplace. Many employers are so afraid of retaliation that they reprimand — or even fire — such "traitors."

This fear extends to the press and the academic world. I read the Israeli press online every day. Despite world opinion against the butchery, nearly all Israeli journalists joined the crowd to support the war. The few who dare to express criticism get death threats; one brave journalist has hired bodyguards.

It angers and sickens me that some Israeli universities also are fomenting the hysteria. Instead of being centers for enlightenment and protectors of academic freedom, two universities have warned faculty, students, and employees that if "extreme" contents are found in their private Facebook accounts, they will be disciplined. At another university, a professor emailed students about a procedural matter and, at the end, added a sentence lamenting the loss of life on both sides in the current conflict. Students complained and the dean threatened the professor with sanctions. At this same university, however, another professor asserted in a public lecture that the only way to deter Hamas is by raping their wives and sisters. When world criticism poured in, the university defended his right to free speech!

Turner — *Is there resistance among progressive and leftist Arabs and Jews?*
Fidel — Yes! I'm very encouraged that 43 Israeli intelligence unit soldiers have refused to serve because of the persecution of Palestinians. Jewish and Israeli Palestinian organizations have united to protest the war. They call for peace on every communication channel available to them.

These protesters always face a mob of extreme right-wing thugs. At first, the police will separate the two groups, but once the thugs start attacking, the police move aside, arrest peace demonstrators, and order them to disperse. In the last month, 1,500 demonstrators were arrested, mostly Israeli Palestinians.

The police actively work to crush peace demonstrations. In one nationwide event, police prevented buses filled with demonstrators from the northern parts of Israel — where most of the Israeli Palestinians live among a larger Jewish population — from entering Tel Aviv. But peace demonstrators are not yielding to the pressure, and many more events are planned.

Turner — *How is the U.S. involved?*
Fidel — Let's be clear: the U.S. government supports the attacks on Gaza.

The Middle East is strategic to the U.S., both economically and militarily. Our government's goal is to keep the area quiet and totally dependent on the United States. Israel serves the purpose handily since it depends on the $3.1 billion of our tax dollars it receives annually. And Congress just approved another $225 million to replenish munitions depleted by Israel's recent bombing.

Decades of brutal occupation by Israel make Palestinians among the world's most revolutionary people. They stand in the way of U.S. dominance and Israel's territorial expansion, which have ethnic cleansing — that is, getting rid of the Palestinians — as a mutual objective.

I remember an interview that Vice President Joe Biden gave a few years ago. He explained, "People should understand by now that Israel is the single greatest strength America has in the Middle East." He asked how many battleships and U.S. troops would have to be stationed there "if there were no Israel."

Aboriginal freedom fighter speaks out against deaths in custody

Alison Thorne

Lex Wotton, is an Australian Aboriginal leader and former political prisoner. He was jailed in 2008 for "riot with destruction," after leading a militant protest against the death of Mulrunji Doomadgee. Doomadgee was arrested in 2004 for talking back to police. A few hours later, he was found dead on the floor of the Palm Island police station with such severe internal injuries that his liver was split in two. Attempts to dismiss this as an accident sparked a righteous community explosion. The following interview was conducted by Melbourne FSP Organizer Alison Thorne just months before an all-white jury found Wotton guilty. After two years in prison, Lex is now free and pursuing a class action lawsuit on behalf of Palm Island Aboriginal people charging the Queensland government with institutionalized racism.

Thorne — *What was your experience growing up on Palm Island, where so many Aboriginal people from across Australia were transported against their will?*
Wotton — I was born on Palm Island in 1967, a product of the Stolen Generation. I lived in Palm Valley near the river. During the summer we'd swim in the creek. We'd hunt freshwater yabbies [crawfish]. We had lots of different bush tucker [native and wild] foods and fruits along the creek.

My Mum's tribe is the Yidingi. They come from near Cairns. She was made a ward of the state, separated from her brothers and sisters and sent to Palm Island. My Mum went into the dormitory system. To get out, she married my father, started a family and had 11 children.

Thorne —*The Palm Island Aboriginal community has a history of resistance. What was your family's involvement?*
Wotton — I recall Mum going to meetings during the '70s. When the Whitlam [Labor] government took office, there were high hopes across the country for land rights for the Indigenous population.

Two of the Magnificent Seven, a group of Palm Islanders who brought action against the government for illegally underpaying them, were my in-laws. They had to line up for rations and were slave labor. Their mistreatment as young kids was shocking.

They struck over their wages. Yeah, that influenced me — I recall when I was a kid watching a re-enactment at school of the strike of 1957. The in-laws used to talk about it, too. So growing up, I knew that things weren't right. I wanted to own my own home, work three days a week and get paid, travel, have a pension and live until I'm old. After 20 years of working hard as a plumber, I have nothing to show for it, because that's the system that we live in.

Thorne — *After the death of Mulrunji, you protested, were arrested and jailed. What led to this?*
Wotton — There was talk in the community that there would be a gathering to discuss his death and try to come up with some answers as to why he died in police custody.

We ended up living under a State of Emergency that should never have been declared.

When I was arrested, I was unarmed and just in a pair of shorts on my veranda. I recall one day sitting in a vehicle with no shirt on and a young lad came up to me and said to me, "Uncle, where were you hit with the stun gun?" I showed him the scars and he asked if it hurt. I told him it did. Then I recalled that he was there when my brother-in-law was arrested in the nude. This young lad and his cousin were playing in the yard, and they were told to hit the ground and had guns pointed to their heads. They were terrorized. My 16-year-old niece was also in the house and they held guns to her head.

> We've witnessed 220 years of domination: the raping of the land, exploitation of Aboriginal art, and a high level of incarceration.

I was targeted as the ringleader of the so-called Palm Island Riots. I am the scapegoat for government inaction and failure to implement the recommendations of the royal commission into Aboriginal deaths in custody.

The recommendations state that, after a death in custody, the suspects should be stood down and removed from the community. They should have nothing to do with the investigation. This did not happen: this man [Chris Hurley], the suspect of a murder, picked up [the investigator at the airport and took him home for dinner. He was a] friend who had formally investigated him before. It was wrong! The same officer that investigated Hurley was also the one arresting us.

If the recommendations of the royal commission had been implemented, it would have made a lot of difference. For example, if the video surveillance was up-to-date, we might have seen a lot more.

Also, if the recommendations had been fully implemented, the deceased wouldn't have been arrested. The coroner touched on that: arrest is the *last* resort, especially in a case of public nuisance.

We need to re-examine the entire case. Let's paint a picture of the flawed investigation and demand answers as to why they didn't follow these guidelines.

Thorne — *What support have you received, and what solution do you see?*
Wotton — Union support for me has been great. There is a history. One of the most famous is the Wave Hill walk-off [1966-1975] when the unions supported our communities. This eventually led to Whitlam handing back some land. Unions and their members are battlers, too, and they stand up for people's rights and have a social conscience. The unions are a voice, and they have to be listened to.

I don't present this issue as being a Black and white issue. There are non-Indigenous people dying in custody, too. It's a social justice issue.

There is also a race of people who have been treated unfairly from 1788 until today. We've witnessed 220 years of domination — the raping of the land, the exploitation of Aboriginal art and the high level of incarceration of Indigenous people. That's exploitation, too. We can't change what happened, but we can recognize what has happened.

We have to stop jailing people for minor offenses, and let's pour money into proper solutions for communities, which will provide services for women and children and help men deal with anger problems, unemployment and low self-esteem.

For the past three-and-a-half years, I have had to put a lot of things on hold and live on hopes. I think positive and will continue to live like that. I want to go forward and have the opportunity to create something better for my people.

Six Nations land claim in Ontario continues to draw widespread support

Ann Rogers

))) The intense standoff near the town of Caledonia between Ontario Provincial Police (OPP) and the Six Nations people protesting the illegal occupation of their land by a developer has eased somewhat. But, says strong Six Nations spokesperson Hazel Hill, a legal and acceptable solution is a long way off.

A fork in the road

The land in dispute is part of the Haldiman Deed granted by the British Crown in 1784 to the Six Nations, or Mohawks, in recognition of their support for England during the American War of Independence. The deed included land stretching six miles on both sides of the Grand River. The Six Nations registered a claim on the land, known as the Plank Road Tract, in 1987, and say that the reserve now covers less than 5 percent of the original holdings. They have never been compensated for tract land sold to non-Natives and have registered 29 land claims during the past several decades. Only one has been settled.

The current dispute arose in late 2005 when the Six Nations determined that they would lose title to the land if they did not stop a housing development being built by developers who obtained ownership of the land illegally.

At the urging of clan mothers, who are part of the Six Nations Confederacy governance system, protesters built a

barricade to halt construction and block off police access.
There is one mother for each clan of the band. Their unique
responsibilities include understanding the clan's spiritual
laws and inherent rights, knowing the language, overseeing
work, and preserving land in trust for future generations.

The Mohawk protesters, with women in the forefront,
stood strong during threats of invasion by the OPP at
Kanenhstaton, the reclamation site near Caledonia. They
took all precautions not to use violent means to keep the
police at bay, despite opposite reports in the racist media. To
use only the truth for protection was a lesson learned from
another Mohawk land claim struggle at Oka, Quebec, in the
early 1990s, where meeting force with force brought blood-
shed on the defenders of the land. The Oka claim has not yet
been settled.

The developers in Ontario, Don and John Henning of
Henco Industries, had received an injunction from the provincial courts ordering the Native occupiers off the disputed
land, known as the Douglas Creek
Estates. When the protesters refused
to leave, Ontario Court Justice David
Marshall issued a contempt of court
order. In the past, Marshall has acted
as a friend to the Six Nations, even
writing a book extolling the people's
humanistic principles, for which he
was awarded an honorary Native title.

The standoff at Kanenhstaton
ended when the province bought out
the developers — paying them almost double the amount
they had invested — and said it would hold the land in trust.
While this ended the confrontation with police, however, it
is not an outcome that the Six Nations agree with. The land
belongs to them, and since the beginning they have asked to

> On the road to
> life, one path will
> lead to harmony
> with the earth,
> and one will lead
> to money and
> greed.

meet and resolve the issue nation to nation with the Canadian government, as stipulated by the Crown when the land was deeded to them.

Even though the developers have now asked the court to set aside the injunction against the protesters, Judge Marshall has vowed to enforce his contempt order and remove the occupiers. Marshall owns land near the Grand River that would probably increase in value if the development were completed.

On Marshall's turn against the Native people he once embraced, Hazel Hill quotes a Hopi proverb: "On the road of life one will possibly encounter a fork in the road. One path will lead to living in harmony with the earth and one will lead to money and greed." She suggests that Judge Marshall has chosen the latter.

Support warmly welcomed

The Six Nations have received a lot of support nationally and internationally, from Natives and non-Natives. One coalition, CommUNITY Friends for Peace and Understanding with Six Nations, has participation from Caledonia residents and many labor unions.

The Mohawks have taken down the barricades, and the racial tensions that erupted during the standoff with racist outsiders and some Caledonia residents have quieted. A group of Six Nations and Caledonia women has started meeting to dialogue on the true history and traditions of the confederacy.

But the struggle is not over. And until the Canadian government gets serious about negotiating in good faith with First Nations people over land claims, it will not be.

Chicanos and the military: Uncle Sam's wars are not our wars!

Moisés Montoya

))) In 1953, four years after coming to the United States from Mexico and getting a job in a cement plant in California, my father received a draft letter from the Army. Though he hardly spoke English, he left his job and freedom behind and entered basic training. As a foot soldier in Korea, side by side with working-class Puerto Rican, African American and white soldiers, Gabriel Montoya was among the post-combat troops guarding and maintaining armaments and supplies for about two years.

My father tells me today that he never believed in the idea of "dying for one's country," whether in Mexico or the U.S. His bi-national reality strengthened his opposition to war based on nationalism and jingoism. "It's wrong," he says, "for one country to attack another one-sidedly, whether it's Korea, Iraq or Afghanistan."

His distaste for serving was only fortified because he had no choice in the matter. He withstood the psychological control of basic training; when ordered to shoot and kill, it was for him "a question of self-preservation, not patriotism." That self-preservation included avoiding being considered treasonous and court-martialed.

He left the Army with no illusions about what he'd gone through and with his skepticism about U.S. foreign policy and the military reinforced.

Less than a decade later, the U.S. invaded Vietnam and began its long, brutal campaign against the Vietnamese people, again in the name of "rolling back communism." Many thousands of Chicanos and Latinos, including two cousins of mine, were drafted.

My cousins were lucky, relatively speaking — they came back alive. Over 47,000 troops never came home; another 153,000 were seriously wounded.

Like most returning combat troops, my cousins both suffered post-traumatic stress disorder and, likely, syndromes related to chemicals like Agent Orange.

Today's troops will inevitably come to realize that U.S. occupation of another people's land is wrong.

Thanks in no small part to massive GI resistance from inside the military machine, Washington was forced to end the war in January 1973. The same day the government signed the Paris Peace Accord, it replaced the draft with voluntary enlistment, hedging its bets on a leaner, meaner killing machine in future wars. From this time onward, the Defense Department has "sold" military service to prospective recruits.

My generation reached service age after Vietnam. As a teen, I wanted to enlist in the Air Force. It sounded exciting, and Uncle Sam dangled opportunities — college money, job training and travel — that my parents couldn't provide. Of course, no recruiter will tell you that war is horrific, that the "ideal" you'll be fighting for is corporate profits, and that those promised benefits may never materialize if you survive.

In the end, I didn't join. I decided the risk wasn't worth it. Like my father before me, I didn't really believe that killing for the U.S. was the right thing to do. And I had another option. In those days, after affirmative action and equal opportunity programs were won, there were college scholarships for low-income students — grants that are uncommon today.

Now earlier gains are gone and times are tougher, making the job of the recruiters easier. The Pentagon spends millions to sign up low-income young people and youth of color — who then fill high-risk, high-casualty jobs on the front lines in Iraq and Afghanistan.

Prime targets for recruiters are Latinos like my nieces and nephews, one of whom has joined the Navy. Latinos make up a fast-growing 16 percent of the population between the ages of 17 and 21 and are increasingly central to the ability of the U.S. to wage war.

The military has historically been the institution where Chicanos, and other racial minorities, have demonstrated their valor and allegiance to Uncle Sam. Besides the training and leadership skills, Latinos have gained social recognition and even citizenship for serving. Even so, over generations the sacrifice has been too great.

And Uncle Sam's wars are not our wars.

My colleague Norma, here in San Francisco, has Chicano friends deployed in Iraq; they enlisted in the Army in the hope that the military service would provide a road to college. They may disagree with what the Army requires them to do, but, they tell her, "It's just a job."

One of her buddies is conducting house searches in Mosul; these raids are a key component of the U.S. effort to stamp out the wholly justified Iraqi resistance against the foreign occupiers. In a recent exchange, Norma told him, "I hope an Iraqi woman hits you over the head with a pan!"

In San Francisco this past November, voters passed a city measure halting military recruitment in public schools and calling for education scholarships and training alternatives to military service. The movement against recruitment is growing.

Young people are part of it. Scores of Latino youth are rejecting the slogan *"Yo soy el Army"* (I am the Army) in favor of *"Yo estoy en **contra** del Army"* (I am *against* the Army). They need and deserve the support of the rest of the Latino community.

So do the troops currently serving. Today's soldiers, sailors, and Marines, like their predecessors in Vietnam, will inevitably come to realize that U.S. occupation of another people's land is wrong. They will see that they have more in common with the darker-skinned people they are interrogating and shooting than they do with the politicians and officers leading a war based on lies and greed.

It is the job of those of us who have lived through many of Uncle Sam's wars to say to our young *hermanas* and *hermanos: Gente,* without you, the U.S. can't maim and drop its bombs around the world. Resist, and we will be beside you.

7. SHAKING IT UP

Time for action, no time to lament

Karla Alegria

My granny was a single mom with nine children ranging from pre-teen to their 30s by the time I came along. Mom was also on her own, with me. They rented a house and together supported the family. Grandma, the expert cook, with her food stand in El Mercado de San Martin, a small city on the outskirts of San Salvador, and my mom with her factory job.

The civil war (1980-1992) was going strong and unionists fought for better pay and working conditions. Texas Instruments shut down its factory, mom lost her job. Work was scarce; it was time for a last resort. For mom, that meant going to the United States to find work to support the family. I was almost five and did not see her again for another four years. In 1989, my aunt and I set out on a road trip to the U.S. She had a toddler and would not see him again until he was 14.

Capitalism blames gay marriage for destroying families. I blame capitalism! Families are separated daily on both sides of the border because of desperate economic conditions created by so-called free trade agreements like CAFTA and NAFTA that benefit only those at the top. In countries like El Salvador it is difficult enough to find work that pays a living wage. Harder if you're older than 35. And forget about it all together if you're a woman over 35.

More and more, the only way out is for people to emigrate to where the jobs are. When they arrive they are often treated as subhuman invaders.

When I first came upon Radical Women (RW) I had only a faint interest in politics. I never expected to learn so much, so fast, about the social conditions and hidden history that affect my daily life — where I come from as a woman, as a Salvadoran immigrant, as a queer person of color. It's impossible to ignore these things once you see them! Three years ago if I'd heard about Nestora Salgado, imprisoned in Mexico, or Marissa Alexander, the African American mother given a 20-year sentence for self-defense, I might have thought, "What a sad story but I can't do anything about it."

> We really do have inalienable rights and it is possible to fight for them — if you are not alone.

Class consciousness was not on my radar then. But *The Radical Women Manifesto* taught me that we really do have inalienable rights and that it is possible to fight for them — if you're not alone.

During a study group on Revolutionary Integration, a founding principle of both RW and our affiliate the Freedom Socialist Party, I learned the true history of the civil rights movement in the U.S. and women's decisive role in it. And became conscious for the first time that I was part of a huge working class.

That's when I grasped that standing up against social injustice like bigotry against immigrants, police violence, and racism was just plain necessary. My activism today comes from a personal sense of responsibility for dispelling the lies that are told to prevent us from uniting against our tiny ruling class that could care less about the most afflicted.

As a person of color and an immigrant, one of the things

I appreciate most about my political involvement with RW and FSP has been the Comrades of Color Caucus — we call it the CCC — which functions within both organizations, nationally. I've learned so much in this caucus. For example, I have legal immigration status and grew up with it. But in the CCC I learned how miserable the lives of undocumented immigrants are, and how pivotal it is for RW and FSP to defend undocumented workers and their families.

Being a woman living under capitalism is tremendously hard. Being a woman of color is very much harder. Analyzing and organizing around these realities, learning and teaching the skills of leadership so necessary for our urgent fight — this is what the CCC does. We are true comrades, of color, loudly denouncing and fighting the brutality of the profiteers, in a country we cannot forget was founded on hundreds of years of racist slavery.

The most important lesson I have learned since becoming an activist is that this is no time to lament! It is a time to unearth our true history as a country and use our power as a class. A time for action!

Lynne Stewart: Can't jail her spirit

Ralph Poynter

In 2005, Lynne Stewart, the intrepid people's lawyer, was wrongly convicted of aiding terrorism for releasing an innocuous press release by a client, Sheik Omar Abdel Rahman, an Egyptian cleric serving a sentence for plotting a 1993 bombing at the World Trade Center.

Radicals and attorneys mobilized in her defense. FSP and RW members attended her trial, organized speaking engagements for her in San Francisco and Seattle, joined her husband Ralph Poynter in a vigil at the White House, and helped organize support rallies. But the prosecution prevailed. Stewart entered prison in 2009 to serve a vindictive 10-year sentence, imposed despite the fact she was 70 years old and suffering from cancer. Happily, on December 31, 2013, after an international campaign calling for early release due to her advanced illness, Stewart was finally released.

The following speech was delivered by Poynter at the October 2012 National Lawyers Guild Conference in Pasadena, California. The Guild is an association of radical and social interest lawyers and legal workers.

Brothers and Sisters, Comrades, Supporters and Friends,

I hope you're not saying Lynne Stewart is just old news. Those of you who know her personally and remember her at these conventions know she will always be a vital force among us. Those of you who were still in high school when she was arrested back in 2002 owe it to yourselves to find out about her, her career, and her case, which is still crucial to all that the Guild stands for.

Let me just say that I am Lynne's husband and a lot prejudiced in her favor. I have lived with her, fought with her and beside her, and loved her for almost 50 years. I want her to be out of prison where she has languished for the last three years. Did I say languish? — Lynne can't languish — she is always the activist, always political, always compassionate. They can't jail her spirit. But we need her out here with us on the front lines!

The federal government locked her up because they wanted to control her defense of Sheik Omar Abdel Rahman and she believed that ethically and morally she had obligations to her client; and that her adversary should not, could not, dictate or curtail what strategy a lawyer must adopt. Maybe you would not have been audacious in the same way Lynne was, in issuing a press release, but she was representing a man who had been subjected to a vicious solitary confinement for many years, was ill, and appeared to be fading. It was "mandatory" to do this to save him. Now that Mubarak has been toppled, Egypt's new president has been calling for the repatriation to Egypt of that client, Sheik Omar. Lynne was right, and the lie has been put to the U.S. government's strident and false claims that her actions somehow contributed to terrorism. And we are still fighting her case — in a petition asking the U.S. Supreme Court to review the lower court's ruling.

Many of you are familiar with the trial and have followed her appeal, and then her re-sentencing, and that appeal. I do want to say that Lynne's case should be important to all criminal defense lawyers and particularly to National Lawyers Guild lawyers because what the government has done to her can happen again. And it can particularly happen to Guild lawyers who regularly take on the cases of people whom the government despises and believes cannot be permitted to win. In essence, using regulations promulgated by the Department of Justice and Bureau of Prisons, Lynne's adversaries attempted to thwart her campaign to keep her client's name alive in Egypt and the world. Her press release to Reuters, not secret, mirrored the many that her co-counsel Ramsey Clark had issued in the face of the same regulations. But they came after her. She is nothing more, or less, than a smart woman with great politics from a working-class background. But her amazing loyalty and relationships with her clients were a threat.

Lynne's case is important for all of you to support because someday you may be confronted in your professional life with a choice between conforming to conduct that pleases the "system," "authority," and doing that which you know to be right and just. Lynne chose her client and her obligation to him, and if you want to increase the safety zone for lawyers centered as she was, you will support her. To be reminded of just who Lynne is, she asked me to read a portion of a speech she gave to the Guild in Minneapolis at the convention there in 2007. It is her credo:

> I believe we have formidable enemies not unlike those in the tales of ancient days. There is a consummate evil that unleashes its dogs of war on the helpless. Our enemy is motivated only by insatiable greed with no thought of other consequences. In this enemy there is no love of the land or the creatures who live there, no compassion for the people. No thought of future generations. This enemy will destroy the air we breathe and the water we drink as long as the dollars keep filling up their money boxes.

We have been charged here, once again, with, and for our quests...to shake the very foundations of the continents. We go out to stop police brutality; to rescue the imprisoned; to change the rules for those who never have been able to get to the starting line, much less run the race, because of color, physical condition, gender, mental impairment.

We go forth to preserve the air and land and water and sky and all the beasts that crawl and fly. We go forth to safeguard the right to speak and write; to join; to learn; to rest safe at home, to be secure, fed, healthy, sheltered, loved and loving, to be at peace with one's identity.

Our quests are formidable. We have in Washington a poisonous government that spreads its venom to the body politic in all corners of the globe. We have wars — big war in Afghanistan, smaller wars in Palestine, Central Africa, Colombia, Kashmir.... Now we have those Democratic and Republican candidates and then an election, with the corporate media ready to hype the results and drown out the righteous protests.

I now need to raise to you the plight of political prisoners in the U.S. (not just because Lynne is one) — numbering more and more Muslims, Earth Firsters, veterans of the 1960s, '70s, and '80s defense of minority communities, resisters, peace activists...brave men and women, held in the harshest conditions, some for more than 40 years. This is more than a worthy focus for Guild lawyers, whose opposition to illicit power should be consistent and militant. Check these folks out at the Jericho Movement and Project SALAM websites. And join their struggles. Many have no legal representation or contact. Even if you correspond, or visit, or join a defense team, or take on one of their cases, your reward will be great — the satisfaction of doing the right thing with people who remain the best among us.

In closing I want to urge you to defend and champion Lynne Stewart, one of our own! Defend and champion all political prisoners! Set her free! Set 'em all free!

Toxic legacy: Native Americans protest deadly fallout from uranium mining

Christina López

Ever since Manifest Destiny infested this green planet, Native Americans fought against the severe exploitation and horrific genocide that powered it. The struggle continues as Indian nations fight to ban uranium mining in their precious homelands.

Uranium mining mushroomed after the launching of the nuclear age. It provides the fuel for the reactors of nuclear power plants. Military demands for uranium, to build weapons of mass destruction, skyrocketed at the end of World War II.

The mining industry got their much sought-after uranium as rich deposits were discovered on Indian reservations in what was originally thought of as desolate, useless land. The mining industry made huge profits off thousands of Native Americans hired to work in the mines at low wages.

But the years of mining eventually wreaked havoc on the reservations of the Navajo, Lakota Sioux, Spokane, and other Native American communities, leaving behind death and disease among tribal members.

Uranium and its lethal dangers

When uranium is mined and milled, it creates radioactive dust and gas that are carried by the winds into the air. Large volumes of contaminated water are also released into rivers and lakes during the process. Throughout the areas surrounding the production of uranium, the many forms of this dangerous debris cause severe health problems and environmental damage.

Because companies failed to install proper ventilation, working conditions for Indian miners turned out to be deadly. As they labored inside the shafts, they breathed in deadly air full of radioactive elements. Their incidences of lung cancer rose at an alarming rate. They also went home covered with the poison, and their families were exposed. Leukemia, bone cancer, and birth defects increased.

On the Spokane Indian Reservation in Washington State, Sherwood and Midnite were two mines operated respectively by Phelps Dodge, the notorious union-buster, and Newmont Mining Corporation, one of the largest mining corporations in the world.

During the years of operation, huge truck transports were used to ship the ore in and out of the mines. The people who lived along the routes had high incidences of cancer. It is in part because of this terrible history that many Pacific Northwest tribes are currently opposing a proposal for a giant new coal transportation port in Washington.

Thousands of mines on Native lands were abandoned during the 1980s when the demand for uranium decreased. Rather than spend money to clean up their ghastly mess, mining companies left behind hundreds of open pits filled with toxic waste for the tribes to deal with. Some of the waste has inevitably leaked into the drinking water and gotten into the food supply.

Environmental racism

Most people know about the partial nuclear meltdown at Three Mile Island in Pennsylvania.

But few people know about the destructive nuclear accident a few months later at a privately owned mine at Church

Native Americans protest outside a conference of uranium-mining interests and federal regulators in Denver, Colorado in May 2010.

Rock, New Mexico, on July 16, 1979. A poorly constructed dam broke, spilling over one hundred million gallons of pooled radioactive waste into the Rio Puerco. The toxins flowed to Arizona and onto the Navajo reservation.

The mine's operator, the United Nuclear Corporation, remained silent right after the accident and failed to notify the Navajo Nation that lives were in danger. After the Centers for Disease Control were called, the indigenous community was finally notified about the radioactive waste seeping into the drinking water used both by people and livestock.

To this day, the corporation has not been fully held accountable for its negligence. It merely paid a small class-action settlement and put a very token amount of effort into cleaning up the mess.

The extent of the damage is appalling. The Church Rock Chapter of the Navajo Nation released a 2007 report describing elevated amounts of radioactive toxins in the affected areas.

Pollution, though, knows no borders. Don Yellowman is president of the organization Forgotten People, which fights for Native sovereignty and for social, environmental, and economic justice. "The water that southern Arizona consumes may be contaminated with radioactive nucleotides from the Church Rock spill," Yellowman warned this reporter. "Indigenous people have been violated for centuries and everyone and every living thing is being poisoned in some form or fashion."

Forgotten People demands immediate action from the U.S. government to remedy the radioactive uranium contamination and compensate its downwind victims.

Native American resistance

For decades, First Peoples have stood strong against the rich and powerful mining industry.

Uniting with other environmentalists, Native resistance to new mining proposals and the buildup of nuclear power plants intensified in the 1970s and '80s. During the 1990s, the Western Shoshone and Paiute led protests to stop a nuclear waste dump on Yucca Mountain. In 2008, the Spokane won a complaint against Newmont Mining Corporation, which was ordered to pay a share of the multimillion-dollar cleanup.

The deadly threat is far from over, however, with the mining industry now lobbying to lift bans and regulations on uranium mining. Their efforts are prompted by the increased demand for uranium by the global nuclear energy industry.

Uranium surpluses are drying up in Europe, and U.S. corporations are looking for ways to commence their highly profitable toxic exploitation once again. Their well-funded propaganda machine is at it once more, cynically trying to convince people that nuclear energy is "safe and sanitary" compared to noxious, climate-change-inducing fossil fuels.

I'm reminded of a merry Disney cartoon that was shown to my class in grade school, which showcased characters from the Magic Kingdom telling us about the promise of atomic power as an abundant and clean source of energy. The film left out, of course, the destructive nature of this energy.

In its goal of finding ways to make buckets of money, the capitalist market system does not plan for disastrous long-term impacts. Without a doubt, the immediate drive for profits has guided the mining industry to disregard the lives of Native Americans, communities of color, and a growing list of poor and working people. Their shortsightedness will impact everyone who lives on this one and only planet of ours for generations to come.

> Years of mining wreaked havoc on Native communities, and pollution knows no borders.

The fight for our Earth is joined. Tribes are still fighting to stop the industry from polluting water and land. In January 2012, the Havasupai won a 20-year ban to stop proposed uranium mines around Grand Canyon. Navajos are currently blocking a uranium transport through their lands.

Environmentalists, or anyone who cares about the air we breathe, can look toward Native Americans, who are standing up against the mightiest of corporations. Indigenous leaders continue to raise awareness on the dangers of uranium mining and the need to safeguard our environment. They are building support and uniting with other environmental and anti-nuclear activists to stop the mining industry from poisoning Mother Earth. This is a battle we must win!

Environmental racism in urban communities of color:
An ecosocialist response

Emily Woo Yamasaki

))) "A world to win, a planet to save!" That theme of the Freedom Socialist Party's 2014 national convention punctuated the urgency of stopping environmental destruction before it makes the earth uninhabitable. Having grown up in San Francisco and lived in New York City for the last 33 years, I have seen the central role of racism in urban ruin. I've concluded that it will take an ecosocialist fight that integrates opposition to race, gender and economic exploitation to get rid of environmental racism.

Race: the determining factor

In 1987, the Commission for Racial Justice of the United Church of Christ (UCC) published a landmark study titled "Toxic Wastes and Race in the United States." It showed that race was *the* single most important factor in determining where U.S. toxic waste facilities were placed. It also found that building these facilities in communities of color was *intentional.*

Its 2007 study, "Toxic Wastes and Race at Twenty, 1987-2007: Grassroots Struggles to Dismantle Environmental Racism in the U.S.," reported that even more people of color were living near polluting sites than 20 years before.

Toxic in New York and San Francisco

My friend Tanya tells a clear story. She is a Black single mother of seven, one an infant. Her family lost their home in the Rockaway Peninsula of New York City through Hurricane Sandy in October 2012. Before Sandy, reports on the need for sea wall reinforcement around NYC went unheeded by city and state officials, and evacuation plans were woefully inadequate. Many of the hardest hit areas were predominantly poor and people of color, including low-income housing projects.

Since the hurricane, Tanya's family has been moved from shelter to shelter in Harlem and the Bronx, miles away from the Rockaways. One shelter was so mouse-infested she was afraid to turn the lights off at night. Illness plagues her kids, but her letters and calls to officials go unanswered.

Duciana, a Radical Women sister and friend, lives in the Bayview-Hunters Point (BVHP) section of San Francisco. Hunters Point is the most polluted part of S.F., contains four times as many toxins as any other city neighborhood, and has asthma, cancer, and infant mortality rates that are among the highest in the state and the country.

By the 1960s, the BVHP neighborhood had become increasingly segregated from San Francisco and today is predominantly African American, Asian, and Latino. In the early 1960s, author-activist James Baldwin said during a visit to the area, "This is the San Francisco America likes to pretend does not exist."

A movement erupts

In the 1960s, while farmworkers rose up against toxic pesticides in California fields and Native Americans pressed for land and fishing rights, people of color in cities protested against incinerators and refineries. Together, they inaugurated the environmental justice movement. In 1967, Black students took to the streets of Houston to protest a city garbage dump that claimed the lives of two children in their community.

Many leaders came out of the civil rights movement, coining the term "environmental racism" and bringing with them the same tactics used in those historic freedom struggles — marches, rallies, petitions, coalition-building, and direct action. The movement has been reinforced by neighborhood action groups and alliances such as those forged between Black and Native American activists who in 1991 organized the First National People of Color Environmental Leadership Summit in Washington, D.C. The principles from that Summit's Declaration helped define the multi-issue demands of today.

The struggle for environmental rights also crosses borders. Yudith Nieto is a native Mexican whose family emigrated to the U.S. after years of drought threatened their way of living as farmers. She is a young organizer with Texas Environmental Justice Advocacy Services (TEJAS), mobilized into action by her family and neighbors in Manchester, the most polluted *barrio* in Houston, who are being sickened by the fumes and pollutants, and threatened with the Keystone XL pipeline.

Women are at the forefront of the movement for environmental rights because they are disproportionately employed in jobs that involve dangerous exposure to toxic chemicals and are therefore afflicted with cancers and miscarriages. For us, the battles against racism and sexism go hand-in-hand. As my friend Tanya says, "It's not just about race. It's also about economics, about education." Ecofeminism, which converges the feminist and ecology movements, has stressed the pivotal links between the exploitation of nature and of women.

What the environmental justice movement must not tolerate is silencing people of color and labeling anyone who makes the link to racism as "divisive." This happened at a January 2014 "Clean Air, No Excuses" rally controlled by white organizers who contended that "race has nothing to do with clean air in Utah." Rebecca Hall, a Black organizer with the group Peaceful Uprising in Utah, forcefully countered, "This is not just an environmental issue. It's an issue of racial justice and economic justice."

Some dismiss the environmental justice movement as a "white movement." Not so. To characterize it as such negates the leading role people of color play in this movement.

An ecosocialist solution

The bitter fact is that racism is a fundamental feature of U.S. capitalism, which relies on the super-exploitation of Blacks and other people of color, and will always put the almighty dollar above the safety and health of our communities. Our planet is in major crisis because of environmental destruction, and the culprits are the super-wealthy one percent. Environmental protection laws under this system are too little, too late, and unenforceable.

Eradicating environmental racism will require openly organizing against capitalism through a grassroots ecosocialist movement. An economic system based on shared abundance instead of private gain, run by the working class rather than the profiteer ruling class, is the only humane alternative to capitalism. Key demands in that direction would include nationalizing the energy industry under workers' control, halting privatization of water and other natural resources, and collective, democratic planning for the needs of people and the earth.

The urgent struggles against racism, sexism and the profit system are inseparable from the environmental movement. Militant organizing that makes these connections is needed now. The very survival of urban communities of color — and the rest of the planet — depends on it.

Still working after 80: Social Security and me

Ann Rogers

For the last 20 years, I have relied on my Social Security pension to pay the basics: electricity, water, phone, supplemental medical insurance (an absolute necessity) and reduced real estate taxes for low-income seniors. But because I unfortunately also need food, clothes, medicine, a car, gas, and car repairs, I still have to have a paying job. All the more so because as the cost of living skyrocketed over two decades, my Social Security did not.

Where did I go wrong? Why at 82, do I not have the means to spend my golden years traveling and living the good life?

It's not like I was sitting around waiting for someone to hand me a living. I was the sole provider when my children were growing up, before and after I became a single parent. This situation is not uncommon; it's the way it is for many families, especially Black, Latino and Native American ones.

My need to keep working has to do with gender disparity and the basic unfairness of the profit system. During my early working years as a waitress, I got rock bottom "traditional" women's pay. Then I went to work at the Sears catalog plant in Seattle at better wages. At first, employee retirement benefits went into a "profit sharing" plan paid in Sears stock. When stock values plummeted in the recession of the late '70s (stop me if this sounds familiar), I lost a lot of my retirement. Only then did Sears start a pension fund.

Then, in 1987, the company closed my plant, putting me

and 500 others out of work. At the age of 60, my prospects of getting a decent paying job were slim. My small Sears pension, unemployment compensation, and odd jobs had to last me till I could get Social Security. Even so, it was only manageable by cashing in what little I could get for the Sears stocks to pay off my home mortgage, car loan and credit card debt. And because I needed a lump sum, the IRS took almost as much as I got!

I was looking forward to collecting my Social Security benefits, thinking that would solve my financial woes. Unfortunately, the changes made to the calculation of benefits have not been to the advantage of retiring workers, especially women. In my case, the highest 30 years of my wages were averaged to figure my benefit. This included the paltry wages I made in the late '50s.

> Social Security is far from broken, but it is barely keeping some of us from extreme poverty.

Now wages are averaged over 35 years, and that is sure to include the low wages most people start out making. For many women, unaffordable childcare means they have to take time off work when their kids are young, and they don't have 35 years' worth of wage history. Guess what a bunch of "zero years" does to the benefit calculation! I was lucky my parents could provide childcare when I needed it.

Women's lower earnings affect women of color the most, not just because we tend to make lower wages, but because more of us are single or heads of households. So we can't get benefits based on a husband's earnings. Of course, the fact that a wife's benefit — half of her husband's — is often larger than what she could get on her own earnings, in itself says a lot about gender inequity!

Needless to say, my benefit was not the financial security

I hoped it would be. I still must work in order to live independently. But I am one of the lucky ones who are physically able to hold a steady job.

And now the experts spout rhetoric about Social Security going broke. The Bush administration's idea of privatizing the system so workers have to invest their retirement in the stock market was scary at the time and even scarier now, after the collapse of banks and businesses.

People who know and tell the truth say that with even modest economic growth, the system should not face a shortfall until more than 30 years in the future. But if Social Security needs bolstering, there's an easy fix. They could eliminate the cap on FICA taxes for high wages; that was already done for Medicare. The Social Security Administration's chief actuary has said that lifting the cap would cover 93 percent of the projected shortfall in revenues for the next 75 years! Instead, we only hear talk of raising the number of work years that go into the benefit calculation to 38 or 40. That would hit women and low-income workers the hardest.

The Social Security system is far from broken. But for some of us, women especially, it barely keeps us out of extreme poverty. It should be made more equitable. I can hear the right wing hollering against *"socialism!"* now. But that's the point. Social Security isn't broken, capitalism is. I hope we do put socialism into practice, and soon!

What's in a name? Dissecting racism and caste oppression

Christine Browning

As a Chicana and socialist feminist activist, I have occasionally encountered other leftists who claim African Americans are members of an economic caste. Even the well-known author/historian Michelle Alexander in her popular book *The New Jim Crow* takes that position. The problem I see is that it places Blacks in an inescapable hierarchical system, rather than being a direct target of capitalist racist oppression, which is surmountable. Members of our Los Angeles Freedom Socialist Party and Radical Women Comrades of Color Caucus recently took up study of this controversy and our investigations helped us to clarify the question.

Even though we live in a country where racism surrounds us daily, it is still a challenge to understand what racism *is*. Is it unique? Is it the same as other forms of domination such as caste or national oppression? What conclusions can we draw from these answers?

The differences between race and nation have been discussed in great detail in writings such as *Revolutionary Integration: A Marxist Analysis of African American Liberation* (Richard Fraser and Tom Boot) and *Viva la Raza: A History of Chicano Identity and Resistance* (Yolanda Alaniz and Megan Cornish). But we're less familiar with the concept of caste. Here, I will look at what a caste is, describe the roots and function of racism, and discuss how racism can be overcome.

Let's start with definitions. *Caste* is "a system of rigid social stratification characterized by hereditary status, endogamy [marriage restricted to within one's caste], and social barriers sanctioned by custom, law, or religion" *(Merriam-Webster)*. The primary example of this is found in traditional Hindu society, where economic class, work and professions are hereditary rankings assigned according to caste.

What about *race?* The *American Heritage Dictionary* uses this definition: "A group of people identified as distinct from other groups because of supposed physical or genetic traits shared by the group. Most biologists and anthropologists do not recognize race as a biologically valid classification...."

Scientifically, there is only one race, the human race. The concept of different races is a social construct used to divide the working class against itself. But the common usage, even among scholars and people of color, is to use the term "race" to describe skin colors, i.e. black, yellow, red, brown.

The differences between racism and caste oppression were laid out by Richard Fraser in a 1984 statement, "On 'Color Caste'," (available at Marxists Internet Archive, www.marxists.org) debating the Spartacist League, a radical group that categorizes people of African descent in the U.S. as a "color caste." Fraser was a Marxist thinker who co-developed the theory of Revolutionary Integration.

This theory grew out of decades-long study of the Black experience and diverged from the position of other activists that U.S. Blacks were an oppressed nationality. Fraser was a founding member of the Freedom Socialist Party, but parted ways over his hostility to the party's feminism. Despite this, his important theory, supported by the Freedom Socialist Party and Radical Women, holds that African Americans are not a separate nation or a caste, but are members of the U.S.

working class who are greatly discriminated against by the institutional and cultural racism that is a main prop of capitalism. For this reason, Black liberation, and freedom for the whole working class, lies in the elimination of capitalism. In this struggle, the leadership of African Americans and other specially oppressed people is decisive to achieving victory.

> Racism was created to justify slavery and perpetuated by capitalism's need to control the working class.

Fraser studied many Black writers in order to understand the nature of African American oppression. He found Black scholar Oliver C. Cox, author of the seminal work *Caste, Class and Race,* to be "absolutely conclusive" in showing that the institution of racism is different from caste. Here are some of Cox's main points from "Race and Caste: A Distinction," a paper published in *The American Journal of Sociology* in 1945:

- "The caste system is ancient, provincial, culturally oriented, hierarchal...and static.... [Economic] production in the caste system is based on hereditary monopoly.... 'Race relations' developed in modern times as our own exploitative system developed. Moreover, race relations...are variants of modern political class problems — that is to say, the problems of exploitation of labor.... The race problem in the United States arose, from its inception in slavery, out of the need to keep Negroes proletarianized."

- "...the individual born of a given race...inherits physical marks which are not only inalienable but also beyond the discretion of the race itself...being born with a given race, there is no alternative but to die within it; in the case of caste no such obdurate rule obtains. In fact, the individual may abandon his caste at will...."

- "In Brahmanic India, there are no half-caste people. A

person is either in a caste or out of a caste; but a person may be half-race or any other fraction of a race."

• "Caste has reference to the internal social order of a society; race suggests a whole people, wherever found about the globe."

• "Probably the most serious objection to the use of the caste belief is that it serves almost invariably to obfuscate the most significant aspects of race relations."

Fraser's study of the nature of race brought the following conclusions:

• The race concept has no biological reality.

• Nevertheless the phenomenon of race exists. Fraser adds, "Proof: try to tell Black people that there is no such thing."

• The reality of race is that it provides the form for social discrimination.

• Race, therefore, is a social relation.

Fraser further concluded that "the racial structure and race relations in the U.S. are historically unique" and that no other society "has ever been founded upon a division based exclusively upon superficial physical characteristics."

Racism, says Fraser, was created to justify slavery and perpetuated "by the requirements of capitalism for the control of the working class: with a united working class capitalism will not survive." But even though racism can reach the extreme of mass insanity, and "however imposing its history and however universally it shapes life and social relations, it is fragile. It will be overthrown with the overthrow of the capitalist class, and only by that."

Tom Boot, a later theorist of Revolutionary Integration, delves more into the question of strategy: "The main historical direction of the Black movement has been revolt against slavery, segregation and discrimination. Despite periodic bursts of intensity, separatism has been a minor and subordinate current.... Blacks and the Black struggle are key to the American class struggle and the American revolution. Hence, Blacks are destined to once again be prime movers in the revolutionary leadership."

At the end of our Los Angeles Comrades of Color Caucus' investigation of the race versus caste question, we had gained a deeper understanding of Radical Women and FSP's position that Blacks, through racism, are oppressed as members of the working class, not as a distinct caste.

It is vital therefore to acknowledge and hold to this basic premise in order to build unity among workers here in the U.S. and throughout our increasingly tumultuous planet. We must throw off the chains and burdens that racist divisions create, and stand strong for each other's rights.

Racial justice and workers' rights

Christina López

))) Growing up in the Southwest, I vividly remember my
parents talking about the United Farm Workers' strike
and how it was embraced by the Chicano Movement. I
remember the rallies and the plea to boycott grapes. I
remember how the United Farm Workers' red and black flag
became a symbol of Chicano pride.

Because of this experience, I naturally equated racial
justice with workers' rights. However, I didn't realize the
role that Black labor had in merging both movements until I
joined a labor history study group sponsored by the Freedom
Socialist Party. There I learned how the fights against slavery,
segregation, and anti-immigrant hysteria have been connected to the fight against low wages, unsafe working conditions
and forced overtime.

This was my real life experience during the 1980s and
'90s in the racist atmosphere in Arizona. Arizona is a "right
to work" state where individuals can abstain from joining the
unions that represent their workforce. As a consequence of
not having strong unions to address discrimination, people
of color get the "preferential treatment" of having the least
desirable, lowest-paying jobs. This was my experience working at the Revlon factory. It was the same when I began
working for the Maricopa County Justice Court system,
where most of the higher-paid managerial positions were
held by whites.

But that was also an exciting time to work for the county
because the workers had just voted to be represented by the

American Federation of State, County and Municipal Employees (AFSCME). Enthusiastically I joined AFSCME, even though I had the "right" not to join. By demand of the union members, AFSCME took on racist, good ol' boy nepotism and low wages by holding demonstrations outside the state and county administrative offices. This got enough publicity to win wage increases and seniority-based promotions. We won by merging the fight for wage increases with the demand to end discrimination.

Powerful history

Because of my experiences, I was fascinated to read *Southern Labor and Black Civil Rights* by Michael Honey. Honey details the labor struggles of the 1930s through the 1950s in Memphis, Tennessee. Prior to the '30s, unions were mostly conservative, craft-based and exclusive to white males. But the '30s ushered in a time of labor insurgency when Black workers united with socialists and communists to push for integrated unions and an end to Jim Crow laws.

The new labor radicals formed the General Council of Riverworkers which represented Black and white workers of the International Longshore and Warehouse Union (ILWU) and the Inland Boatmen's Union. The Council strove to end the racial-economic system of Southern apartheid that crushed union strikes. Learning from the mistakes of the past, the Black and white dockworkers organized jointly and emerged victorious in a 1939 strike along the Mississippi Delta. This incurred the wrath of conservative union leaders who cooperated with the Memphis business establishment in smashing the progressive unions.

Such defeats brought the Southern labor movement to a crashing halt by the 1940s. But not everything was lost. Some of the Black leaders eventually went on to spearhead the civil rights movement of the 1950s and '60s. They took the lead in making revolutionary integrationist demands for equality for all humans in every aspect of life including fair housing, equal opportunity employment, education, and political activism. Revolutionary Integration is the hallmark theory of the Freedom Socialist Party that states that the historical tendency of African Americans has been toward equality and integration, not separation, and that the fight to end racism threatens the very foundations of capitalism and pulls the whole working class forward.

Building labor's fight now

Today it is even more true that in order to survive, the labor movement needs to be involved in fighting discrimination, because the majority of today's labor force is women and people of color. Unions need to address our issues in order to grow.

Yet discrimination still exists in our unions. Often this is because union leaders are trying to appease the Democratic Party rather than rock the boat by militantly defending affirmative action or confronting racist practices. But this dysfunctional party's interests are not with labor but with big business.

Has affirmative action had a positive impact? *Yes!* I am very grateful it was won. It is a necessary reform that has tremendously empowered all labor — especially Black labor. This is why civil rights activists led by Black workers fought so hard to gain and keep it. This is also the reason the right wing, from the beginning, has worked so hard to weaken it.

The good news is that because the workplace is more integrated, partially due to affirmative action, rank-and-file union members are pushing organized labor to take a more militant stand on social issues.

• Boeing, Microsoft and other multi-nationals felt a powerful kick in the ass by the international working class when it showed its might protesting the World Trade Organization in Seattle in 1999.

• The same year, the ILWU successfully organized a West Coast work stoppage on behalf of Mumia Abu-Jamal, an outspoken Black radical and political prisoner who was then on death row and is still serving a life sentence. The work stoppage coincided with a Millions for Mumia rally in San Francisco where I witnessed 25,000 people give a standing ovation to rank-and-file longshore workers on the stage. Mumia has strong labor support because he showed solidarity with strikers at ABC News Network by refusing to be interviewed by scab reporters.

• The powerful impact of labor was also felt by white supremacists in the Northwest when the Martin Luther King County Labor Council sponsored a protest of a racist rally held in Enumclaw on July 4, 1999.

These demonstrations happened as a direct result of a multiracial alliance of working-class activists pushing to get labor on board.

Martin Luther King understood the race-class connection when he said:

> Not logic, but a hollow social distinction has separated the races. The economically depressed white accepts his poverty by telling himself that, if in no other respect, at least socially he is above the Negro. For this empty pride in a racial myth he has paid the crushing price of insecurity, hunger, ignorance, and hopelessness for himself and his children.

Racism and all the social injustices that come with it (poverty, the prison-industrial system, police brutality, etc.) will not end until we — the working class, *las compañeras y los compañeros* — look beyond the barriers of discrimination built by the big-time bosses and see that the solution to economic disparity is to overthrow capitalism.

It is a system that relies on competition — where the majority of the world's wealth benefits one to two percent of the population. What we need is *cooperation* — where the world's resources are shared by everyone and the needs of "those people" become *my* needs and all of our needs. For white workers that means acknowledging the "hollow distinction" of white privilege and accepting the leadership of people of color. For people of color that means we have to recognize and stand up to racism, and acknowledge that the profit system, rather than white people, is the root of the problem.

I urge you to get involved. Join the fight against police violence. Form a rank-and-file caucus to push your union. Stand up to discrimination in the workplace. Or join organizations such as Radical Women and the Freedom Socialist Party. This is what will make our movements powerful.

State budget crises call for a united response by labor unions and communities

Nancy Reiko Kato

Rickii Ainey, homebound in New Orleans with arthritis, is fighting desperately to keep her Medicaid-funded personal care assistant. Four years ago, she got in-home aid after she tried to commit suicide. Now, the state of Louisiana is planning to institutionalize Ainey, and 11,000 other poor, disabled people as a money-saving "solution" to a $1.6 billion budget gap.

Ainey's story is the tip of an iceberg. Millions of U.S. residents are confronting equally devastating scenarios as states close a collective $140 billion shortfall — by unraveling the nation's social fabric.

The state budget gaps seem mammoth. In truth, they are chump change compared to what the federal government spends on tax breaks for the rich and bloody military occupations. Obama's tax cut extensions for the rich cost $68 billion per year. The Iraq and Afghanistan wars another $170 billion. Those billions could save every state.

At the state level, politicians add insult to injury. New Jersey Governor Christie vetoed a tax on millionaires. Wisconsin Governor Walker offers tax breaks to businesses that move to his state, even though it's broke.

In short, while Corporate America is ringing up near record profits, (an annual rate of about $1.6 trillion) ordinary folks suffer tax/fee hikes, shrinking paychecks, and service cuts.

Organized labor has looked to Democrats to stop this

massive theft of wealth from the working class. But both parties are equally guilty.

Let's make the bosses pay for their crisis.

Cuts that kill

A main target of budget cuts is the safety net that helps people of poor and modest means survive. Many programs, already slashed to the bone, now face elimination.

Texas, which ranks 49th in the U.S. for mental health spending, plans to cut $134 million more. Oklahoma is making more reductions to its child abuse prevention programs. Georgia is downsizing staff who help people apply for food stamps and Medicaid.

Massachusetts dumped a health program for poor immigrants, and cut six percent from HIV/AIDS prevention. Kansas eliminated dental services to seniors and people with disabilities. Michigan, with the top unemployment rate, slashed "No Worker Left Behind" by 38 percent. This program had enabled 75 percent of participants to find jobs!

Hiking higher-ed costs is another popular move. This, despite tuition costs rising *500 percent* from 1983 to 2008! Florida is raising university tuition by 32 percent over two years. In Minnesota, 9,400 students lost financial aid grants.

Public schools are equally under siege. Arizona slashed funding for kindergarten programs by half and Colorado is spending $400 less per student.

Open season on unions

To hear right-wing pundits tell it, states are bankrupt because of "overpaid public workers."

Just two years ago, national furor was correctly directed at Wall Street, large banks and big business. But capitalist politicians and news outlets are working overtime to redirect outrage at public-sector unions. This campaign is captured in union-busting attacks, such as those by Ohio Governor Kasich, who wants to ban unionization for 14,000 childcare and homecare staff, and fire state workers who strike. Or Wisconsin Governor Walker who plans to eliminate the right of government workers to form unions.

Neoliberalism is the economics behind this assault. It's a strategy for maximizing profits for corporations on a global scale, and privatization of public services is key. What better way to accomplish this than to bankrupt government in the process of bailing out big business?!

With politicians and bosses aiming at the public sector, organized labor must either fight or die.

Democrats and Republicans are "redesigning" government while capitalist economists talk about the "new normal" of "post-recession" America. So far, there appears to be no bottom for how ugly that new reality will be for the U.S. working class. With the politicians and bosses aiming their nukes at the public sector, organized labor has two options: fight or die.

The good news is that labor can still fight and win if it reaches out and builds alliances with the community — now. As the organized expression of the working class, labor has the capacity to mobilize the masses. Likewise, the masses have self-interest in allying with labor.

The AFL-CIO (American Federation of Labor - Congress of Industrial Organizations) spent over $200 million in the 2010 elections to reach 17 million union members. But this money was wasted on Democrats. Instead, just imagine redirecting all that energy into building a labor/community alliance to save public services.

Rank-and-file unionists can't wait for top officials to set this into motion. Leadership must come from the bottom, through worker-radicals of all stripes.

An example of this is in Washington State, where Sisters Organize for Survival, a campaign initiated by Radical Women, has petitioned the State Labor Council to "mobilize a mass labor/community rally against budget cuts."

Make global revolt the "new normal"

On every continent, workers are using general strikes to combat austerity measures. U.S. labor also has a history of using general strikes to fight, and it's time to employ this weapon again.

With union membership only a fraction of the workforce, the AFL-CIO and the Change to Win Federation need to reach the entire working class. A demand to do this is "30 for 40." Popularized by socialists in order to create new jobs during the Great Depression, this slogan addresses the lack of jobs. As today's Great Recession winds on, the demand of *30 hours work for 40 hours pay* makes total sense. After all, workers' productivity has risen *400 percent* since 1950.

Some might say that "30 for 40" is too pie-in-the sky. And it's true that bosses often threaten to move jobs when workers get too uppity. But workers are uppity everywhere these days.

To put Corporate America on the hook, and win 30 for 40, a double punch is needed of general strikes on the home front and international solidarity with striking workers in other countries to raise standards globally.

Thanks to work stoppages and mass protests from Greece to Tunisia, things are looking promising. The U.S. has been slow to join this global revolt, but a spark from labor could quickly fire things up.

8. IN THEIR FOOTSTEPS

In the candidate's own words:
Why I am running as a socialist feminist

Christina López

Christina López was the Freedom Socialist Party's candidate for U.S. vice-president in a national write-in campaign with presidential candidate Stephen Durham in 2012.

I used to be a registered Democrat. But I gave that up during the Clinton years, when the Democrats and their Republican cohorts dismantled welfare and passed the North American Free Trade Agreement, with its devastating effects for workers here and abroad. The parties together also passed laws to imprison people for much longer. The Democrats say they represent the common people, but their actions say otherwise, and it goes against my interest as a working-class Chicana to support them.

I didn't switch to the Republicans because in Arizona, where I grew up, party leaders were viciously going after people of color and immigrants. Instead, I went through a prolonged period of blissful apathy before joining the Freedom Socialist Party. The party's optimistic outlook for solving economic inequality and hardship by getting rid of capitalism made sense.

Now I am running for U.S. vice-president as a Freedom Socialist candidate because the state of this "golden land of opportunity" is ever so depressing. We have got to step up the resistance.

Growing poverty is alarming. So are the out-of-control costs for healthcare, food, shelter, and education. The incarceration rate for the poor and people of color is exploding. The assault on reproductive freedom is stripping women of basic rights. The detentions, raids, and deportations of immigrants are abominations — as are the multiplying U.S. wars.

I could go on and on. But the point is things need to change and it is urgent that they do. Yet the Democrats and Republicans compound the problem with policies that will make the rich richer via more mega tax breaks or corporate bailouts.

And what have they done for the non-rich? Another reason I am running is all the cuts to education and social safety net programs.

My parents relied on welfare, food stamps, and public housing to get by. Without it, my brothers, sisters, and I would have had unstable, chronically homeless childhoods. My mother was able to take advantage of a job creation program for welfare recipients that allowed her to go to nursing school and leave welfare behind.

If my mother had to rely on welfare now, we would be in desperate straits, because today we have neither real welfare nor effective programs to escape poverty. I say let's bring them back. No more cuts!

Where will the money come from? Let's begin by taxing corporate profits, ending all wars, and diverting Pentagon funds to pay for social needs. Let's end the politicians' strategy of pitting elders and the younger generation against each other for economic resources. Instead, let's put seniors and youth, together, in charge of the budget!

Every four years this sham gets played out where we are asked to vote for change but, in reality, everything remains the same — or gets worse. The Durham-López campaign offers a chance to vote for what you deserve.

Norma Abdulah: Remarkable Harlem revolutionary

Jennifer Laverdure

Norma Abdulah is a proud member of Radical Women in Harlem, New York City. A unionist and a radical, she has always been moved by the promise of liberation and has lived her life as an agitator for workers' and women's rights and Black freedom.

Laverdure — *Where did you grow up?*
Abdulah — I was born in Harlem in New York in 1921. I lived in a tenement with my parents and three brothers. I am African, East Indian, Chinese and French.

My father was educated at the Queen's Royal College in Trinidad as a certified public accountant and secretary. When he went to seek employment as a public accountant in New York City, he was told that he was "applying for a white man's job, not a Negro job." Instead he was given a job as an elevator operator, where he was responsible for emptying large, heavy trash cans. On his first day he collapsed while trying to lift the trash cans.

Black men were expected to do strenuous manual labor, but my father couldn't. So he stayed at home.

My mother was a domestic. She cooked and cleaned and sometimes baby-sat in the evening. At times she would come home as late as 2:00 in the morning, traveling home all alone on the subway.

Laverdure — *What was it like with your father at home?*
Abdulah — It was great. He took my brothers and me to all

the places of culture we could afford. The Metropolitan did not sell opera tickets to Black people. But my mother was part Chinese and kind of light-skinned, and they thought she was buying the tickets for her boss.

> If women want humanity to progress, they must take a leadership role.

My father, brothers and I would climb the steps up high to the inexpensive seats in the Family Circle and watch the opera from there.

From where we lived, we could see the Low Memorial Library of Columbia University that seemed to reach the heavens. My father always used to say that he yearned for at least one of his children to enter that great edifice of learning and earn a degree.

I said to myself, "I'm going to do that."

Laverdure — *What was your education like?*
Abdulah — In the early 1930s we moved from Black Harlem to Spanish Harlem, a working-class area of white immigrants from places like Russia and Yugoslavia and of Spanish-speaking Cubans and Puerto Ricans.

Going to school in Spanish Harlem, I was the darkest student in my class. They put me in the low-performing class. I rebelled. I said, "I'm not going to do any work."

My mother said, "What?! If you don't do the work they will assume they are correct, that you *can't* do the work. You go there and show them — move to the top of the class!"

That's what I did.

They moved me up in the system of classes, and I was placed in the rapid-advance class. I later took an exam to attend Hunter High School. I completed my undergraduate studies at Hunter College in 1943.

I then entered Columbia University's graduate program in philosophy and science.

Laverdure — *And you were the program's first Black woman?*
Abdulah — I was the only violet among the lilies. I was the only person of color in the program. The other students liked me and invited me to become a member of the Philosophical Society, of which I became secretary. I was invited to present a paper. I chose as my subject "Historical Materialism: A Scientific Way of Studying Human History and Society."

At the time, I was a member of the Communist Party. I invited people who I thought were my comrades to support me when I presented this paper. They came. But when I got up and started to present, one of the women from the Communist Party got up and said, "Your job is to speak to the Negro problem!" And she stormed out, with the other party members following her.

I was flabbergasted! Given my topic, I didn't expect the other white students to support me, but I thought my comrades would.

I pulled myself together and went ahead with my talk, but I was very low in my heart. I thought, "What did I do wrong? Why did they behave like that?" From then on, I disassociated from the Communist Party.

Still, I continued to read about the Soviet Union fighting Nazism and providing free education to the people. Communism was the best answer being presented to the problems of capitalism.

Laverdure — *What were your experiences after becoming a grade school teacher in the New York public school system?*
Abdulah — I talked to the other teachers about organizing a union, because all we had back then was the National Education Association, which would only go as far as advocating for teachers to receive sick pay. At first, my colleagues said, "We are professionals, not blue-collar workers." They called me unpatriotic and a dirty communist.

But I educated the students about the need for a union, who then debated with their teachers. In 1967, we won the right to unionize from city government. We formed the United Federation of Teachers!

Laverdure — *Did you become an officer in the union?*
Abdulah — They completely ignored me. There was no recognition of Black women's contributions to the union even though we fought for it. But I said, "My conscience is clear, I did the right thing."

Laverdure — *What has been your involvement in politics since then?*
Abdulah — I continued to work in the union. I was active in the civil rights movement. My name is inscribed in the Southern Poverty Law Center building in Montgomery, Alabama. The inscription is a tribute to my contributions in the struggle for people of color to be accepted as first-class citizens in this country.

I worked with organizations on the Left. And I traveled to China to learn about and support the revolution there.

Laverdure — *What advice do you have for women of color fighting for justice today?*
Abdulah — I would tell them that no progress is made without struggle. They are not the first to help to make this a better world, and they will not be the last. But they will be among the greatest.

It is important to understand historical development so we know that what we are enjoying today is the result of others having struggled and sacrificed. Women today must understand that struggle is an integral part of living.

In Radical Women, I continue the fight for human liberation. I can express myself there and get respect for my ideas.

I have been able to present on the contributions of African Americans to the Harlem Renaissance. I have always felt a certain freedom of participation in Radical Women.

To me, Radical Women represents the future of human development. Joining us will give women an historical understanding of their role and the role they need to play in the future. If women want humanity to progress, they must take a leadership role. I encourage all women to get involved with us!

Life and times of the multifaceted Ann Rogers:
Native American feminist, anti-fascist and unionist

Christina López

Ann Rogers is an active Chippewa (also known as Ojibwe) member of the Freedom Socialist Party and Radical Women in Seattle and a mentor in the National Comrades of Color Caucus of the two organizations. A writer for the FREEDOM SOCIALIST on Native issues, Rogers has represented FSP and RW in support work for American Indian Movement activist and political prisoner Leonard Peltier. She was also one of the founders of United Front Against Fascism, launched in 1988, which successfully organized a broad movement to oppose white supremacists who were trying to win young Nazi skinheads to the cause of turning the Pacific Northwest into an all-white enclave.

Rogers was interviewed by her Chicana-Apache NCCC compañera Christina López.

López — *You didn't learn that you were Chippewa until later in life. Can you tell me about this?*
Rogers — My Native heritage comes from my father. He was the oldest of 12 children born to a Chippewa mother and a Scottish immigrant father near her reservation at Hayward, Wisconsin. He was sent to live with his uncles in Nebraska at the age of 12 and moved to the West Coast with them shortly after.

Because of the intense racism against Indians during that

period and because they did not belong to Northwest tribes, they chose to blend in with the white population, a decision my father followed the rest of his life.

When one of my sisters read a newspaper story about one of his cousins being a leader in a Native church, she asked my dad about it. She recognized the name from his stories about his uncles and cousins. Only then did he tell us that his mother was Indian. By this time I was married with school-aged kids, who were elated to learn of their Indian heritage.

I found it easy to identify with Native culture. When my tribe wanted to get back land that my sisters and I owned by inheritance, they contacted us. Only then did we know we had inherited it. We promptly gave it back to them.

In 1989, one of my sisters and I went back to visit the Lac Courte Oreilles reservation, home to my grandmother and her mother. While we were in Wisconsin, I participated in a protest by my tribe against white racists who were attacking the tribe's sovereign spearfishing rights. The protests were ultimately successful.

López — *You were born in 1926. How did the Great Depression affect your family?*
Rogers — Our family rented a farm, raised dairy cows and sold milk. My dad worked at another dairy close by and my mother hired out as cook and housekeeper for those who could still afford it. She also sold baked goods, which she delivered in our Model A Ford pickup. We were able to raise most of our food, but money for rent and clothes was scarce.

López — *During World War II you worked at Boeing. What did you do there?*
Rogers — I got the job at Boeing right after graduating from high school. I was a machinist. I drilled the holes in wing

panels that the riveters put the rivets in. We were all very proud of what we were doing. Boeing made sure we knew we were making excellent planes that were really needed in the war effort — I wasn't critical of the U.S. motivation for being in the war then, which I am now.

It was the kind of work I liked to do. And people had money and were getting out of Depression poverty. Most men were off fighting the war, so they needed women to fill in the workforce.

Lópe z — *What happened when the war ended?*
Rogers — Like a lot of Rosie the Riveters, I was laid off.

Lópe z — *What challenges did you face as a single working mother raising three children?*
Rogers — The biggest challenge for me was the same as it is for most working mothers — how to feed, clothe and house a family on the wages women are paid. Finding the time to interact with your kids and to give them the guidance they need is also a challenge.

Lópe z — *How did you meet Radical Women?*
Rogers — At my Sears warehouse job, I was a member of Teamsters Local 130 and a shop steward. I was elected to be a rank-and-file contract negotiator three times by the workers. I went to a labor forum because I was looking for some information that would help me in negotiations. I met Radical Women outside that forum handing out flyers for their events.

RW was heavily involved in women's health clinic defense work at that time. It was also involved in getting women into good union jobs, both traditional and non-traditional. These were some of the reasons I joined Radical Women.

I also liked RW's history of being a strong supporter of

Native rights. Along with FSP, RW had helped the Puyallup Tribe reclaim Cascadia, which had been an Indian hospital but was taken over by the state for a youth detention center. The co-founders of RW, Clara Fraser and Gloria Martin, were the most compassionate and intelligent women I had ever met.

López — *What moved you to become a revolutionary socialist feminist and join the Freedom Socialist Party?*
Rogers — Watching the destruction of the environment and personal freedoms on top of working people's struggle to survive, it was evident to me that this downward spiral was not going to end under capitalism.

López — *Did the fact that FSP and RW have a joint Comrades of Color Caucus affect you?*
Rogers — Yes, although I wasn't aware at the time that a caucus of members of color was a unique thing for a left group to have.

I see the caucus as a body that can help FSP and RW strategize on how to intervene in the progressive movements of people of color. The CCC's role should be to keep informed about and involved in these movements, and to help show other activists the value of joining the party and RW.

López — *You were a leader in the United Front Against Fascism. What was it like to be part of that anti-racist movement?*
Rogers — It was very encouraging to see the number and diversity of the communities that joined us in that fight. All had either lived through or learned about the Nazi regime in Germany and were going to make sure it did not happen here. United Front Against Fascism did curb the neo-Nazi recruitment effort in the Northwest and sent their organizer packing to the South.

López — *The Nazi movement is growing in Europe today. Do you think it could do the same here?*

Rogers — Definitely. As the economy deteriorates and money gets tighter, it could happen here. The American Nazi Party has been in existence most of my life. And in my opinion the political ideology of some other ultra-right groups is not far from fascism.

López — *How can we stop it?*

Rogers — As long as capitalism runs our government, the far-right movements will be key players. We can hit the streets in mass protests to get some reforms, as people have done in the past here and around the world. But only the revolutionary fight for a socialist society and government will stop the fascist movement for good.

López — *If you could give today's young activists one word of advice, what would it be?*

Rogers — How about five words? Join the revolutionary socialist movement.

Pepe Palacios:
A proud gay resistance
fighter speaks out

Stephen Durham

Pepe Palacios is a member of the Movement for Sexual Diversity in Resistance (MDR), a Honduran lesbian, gay, bi and transgender organization. He is on the steering committee of the National Front of Popular Resistance, a broad coalition formed to oppose the government of Porfirio Lobo, who took power in the 2009 U.S.-backed coup d'état that ousted elected president Manuel Zelaya.

During a U.S. tour sponsored by Chicago's Gay Liberation Network in 2013, Palacios publicized MDR's campaign to demand justice for the 91 LGBT people who have been murdered in Honduras since the coup. Palacios was interviewed by Stephen Durham, a longtime gay activist and the Freedom Socialist Party's U.S. presidential candidate in 2012.

Durham — *What is the history of the LGBT movement in Honduras? And what changes did the coup bring to the lives of gay people and their organizations?*
Palacios — The LGBT movement started in the mid-'80s, largely in response to HIV/AIDS. These early organizations did remarkable work fighting HIV/AIDS in our community. They evolved from gay social clubs into NGOs, and focused on their own fight and weren't aware of the other struggles going on around them by feminists, indigenous and Afro-Hondurans, union workers, and young people.

These NGOs became dependent on international development funds allocated exclusively to fight HIV/AIDS. As a result, even LGBT human rights demands were left out of their agendas.

In the beginning of Manuel Zelaya's presidency, conditions for gays were similar to what they had been under previous rightist governments. But in 2008 the unrest that was sweeping across Latin America, the "socialist wave," came to Honduras and Zelaya, too, shifted to the left.

> When Zelaya's government was overthrown, LGBT people were in the streets demanding democracy. That was our "Stonewall."

Before the coup, President Zelaya asked LGBT organizations to support his campaign for a constitutional assembly. Most groups said yes, because Zelaya's initiative offered an unprecedented opportunity to gain visibility and become part of a larger social movement that called for a new, inclusive constitution. So when Zelaya's government was overthrown, LGBT people were in the streets from day one, demanding the restoration of democracy. That was our "Stonewall" — when we said "no more!"

Durham — *You are a co-founder of the Movement for Sexual Diversity in Resistance (MDR). How and why did your organization form?*

Palacios — From its inception, the National Resistance Front invited LGBT organizations to join the steering committee. However, the coup regime responded with a wave of violence and 26 LGBT people were killed in seven months, including a well-known gay leader and resistance activist, Walter Tróchez. As a result, LGBT organizations decided to reduce their visibility and activism, and many abandoned their seats in the Resistance Front.

They didn't understand that it was a historic and unique opportunity to finally advance the gay movement beyond its narrow focus on fighting HIV to a broader struggle for social justice and equality for all.

MDR was born "officially" in October 2010 by a group of LGBT activists who were socialists and resistance supporters. Many of us had been active in, or even founders of, gay NGOs. But when those agencies retreated, we decided to form a left-wing LGBT political organization. Our goal was to demand equal participation within the Resistance Front and to become a recognized voice that could fight for justice for all the hate crimes and assassinations against our LGBT community — but also support the struggles of all the social groups in resistance.

Durham — *Can you describe the role of MDR activists in the resistance movement against the government of Porfirio Lobo and in the upcoming Honduran national elections in November 2013?*

Palacios — We have never recognized the government, not just because of the coup, or the impunity with which murders of LGBT people continue; there are other reasons as well.

In 2004, when Porfirio Lobo was the Speaker of the House, he promoted a change to the constitution that specified that marriage be between two persons of the opposite sex. He also called for reinstatement of the death penalty. One month later Porfirio Lobo won the nomination of his party with support from churches, conservatives, and the wealthy elite. However, Zelaya defeated him in the presidential elections the following year.

In 2012, the Resistance Front created its own electoral party and in the primary elections we had a gay man and a transgender woman running for congress. They didn't win, but it was a major advance for the LGBT community. For the November 2013 elections, the resistance presidential candidate was Xiomara Castro, Zelaya's wife and the former first lady.

Durham — *The Obama administration says that respect for gay rights is now a factor in its foreign policy decisions. It has even sent FBI agents to Honduras to help prosecute cases of murder against gays — cases that the U.S.-backed government has refused to investigate. Can you explain this contradictory policy?*

Palacios — For Obama, support for LGBT rights is synonymous with votes. He won the 2012 elections because of gay and Latino voters. So I'm not sure if Obama's position is real and sincere. I think the FBI was sent down to work on gay murder cases due to pressure by human rights organizations, but also to protect Obama's image among gay voters and to clean up the image of this repressive and homophobic government. The level of violence in Honduras is the highest in the world: 85.5 murders per every 100,000 inhabitants.

The Obama administration said publicly that they were against the de facto regime that was installed, but we now know that the U.S. State Department knew about the plans to overthrow Zelaya. The plane that took Zelaya away first landed at the Palmerola U.S. military base in Honduras before proceeding on to Costa Rica.

Durham — *When you spoke at Columbia University in New York, I was impressed to hear you describe yourself as a socialist and feminist. How do you see those ideologies intersecting, and do many other gay and left activists in Honduras share your perspective?*

Palacios — "If socialism is not feminist, there's no socialism." That's not just a phrase, but also an absolute truth. Patriarchal culture has built a heterosexist and masculine society.

If we don't dismantle the patriarchy we can't guarantee that we'll have an equal and just society. So that must be one of the goals of any serious socialist movement.

Unfortunately, the patriarchy has permeated all social groups, even LGBT organizations, most of which are "G" organizations. They reproduce the *machista* culture: lesbians are treated as second-class citizens (as are all women in our society), and the trans population is treated the worst of all. Today there are few activists or leaders that share MDR's socialist and feminist perspective, but our numbers are increasing.

Women of the world — resist, protest, fight!

Nestora Salgado

This International Women's Day statement was issued by indigenous leader Nestora Salgado from her Mexican prison cell in Tepic, Nayarit on March 7, 2014. Salgado is a naturalized U.S. citizen and, at the time of her arrest, she was the coordinator of an elected community police force, authorized under the Mexican constitution.

While carrying out her duties in her hometown of Olinalá, Guerrero, Salgado angered corrupt officials with ties to local criminals who ordered her arrest on federal kidnapping charges. She was transferred to a maximum security prison hundreds of miles from Olinalá, denied access to her attorneys and visits from her family, and held in conditions amounting to torture.

The Committee for a Revolutionary International Regroupment (CRIR) launched a coordinated campaign to free Salgado on Human Rights Day 2013. The Freedom Socialist Party, a member of CRIR, launched the fight in the U.S. after getting in touch with Nestora's husband and daughters who live near Seattle, Washington.

Together with her family and Radical Women, the FSP kicked off the Libertad para Nestora/Freedom for Nestora campaign with committees in Seattle, New York City and Los Angeles. These committees joined internationally coordinated efforts in Mexico, the Dominican Republic, Costa Rica, Australia, Brazil and Argentina seeking the release of Sal-

gado and the many other political prisoners incarcerated in Mexico for organizing self-defense against corrupt state and federal police forces and criminal syndicates.

My name is Nestora Salgado García. I am 42 years old and have three daughters and four grandchildren. I have been unjustly jailed since August 21 of last year. Even though I am jailed and my captors want to break me, I speak to you with optimism on this International Women's Day 2014.

This is a message to the women of Mexico and the United States, as well as the women of other countries where women suffer discrimination.

My message is to resist, to protest and to fight whenever you find yourself humiliated in your place of work, your community or even in your own home.

The life of women in countries such as Mexico is very difficult, above all in *campesina* (peasant) families and communities like mine in the mountains of Guerrero, a state which has always had a lot of poverty and inadequate levels of all types of services. Guerrero also has suffered a lot of corruption and abuse at the hands of government officials.

I have always worked to maintain my daughters, the first of whom was born when I was 16 years old. I had to emigrate from Mexico to the United States where I worked doing many things like cleaning houses and working as a waitress in restaurants. Through my own efforts, I managed to become a U.S. citizen. But I never forgot my roots, my parents, my brothers and sisters, and my family who I frequently visited. Neither did I forget my community. I could not remain indifferent to what was taking place with my neighbors and in my hometown of Olinalá, which unfortunately was happening in other places in our cherished Mexico.

The abuses of organized crime had become common-place every day. It had become impossible to live in peace. We could not leave our houses. We could not work, travel, mount a business or confidently send our children to school. We could not go to the town square in peace and enjoy an ice cream. So, the community suddenly organized itself and elected me as its representative. I became the coordinator of Olinalá community police.

In the beginning, the government officials supported the community police. The governor of Guerrero provided us with two vehicles and other support. We also received official documents designating us as community police.

As the community police, we did our job and we did it well. We served the community of Olinalá. We confronted organized crime and those who supported it. In the first year, the index of major crimes dropped by 90 percent. Maybe this is why the government ended up attacking us and taking me into custody together with 12 other CRAC (Regional Coordination of Community Authority - Community Police) in Guerrero.

I was arrested in an impressive display of military and police force, greater than any used previously in apprehending the worst drug traffickers. Within hours, I was sent to a high security prison in Nayarit where I am currently held as if I were a dangerous animal.

I am isolated from all the other inmates. One of my daughters and one of my sisters can only visit me every two weeks. I cannot speak to anyone. I never see the sun or enjoy sunshine. I receive none of the pain medication I need due to a car accident I suffered. I am allowed no magazines or newspapers. I cannot even receive a letter from my husband who is in the United States, nor a drawing from one of my grandchildren. I am allowed only a few minutes of con-

Talking Back contributor Miriam Padilla (*second from right*) and other participants at a Freedom for Nestora rally outside the Mexican consulate in Seattle on Human Rights Day, December 2013.

versation with my daughter Saira. I cannot watch television.

I know they want to break me but this will not happen. I know that in locking me up they want to send a message to all the women and men in Mexico standing up against injustice. But they will not break me. I will never ask for forgiveness from my jailers. I have no reason to ask forgiveness from anyone, especially the Mexican government. Out of my mouth and from my heart, you will hear only words of encouragement for all those who, like me, have committed themselves to accomplishing something for their communities and their families.

I want to speak especially to the women — to the wives and the mothers of the other imprisoned members of the community police. I say we will endure the cold prison. And we believe that the day is near when we will be free.

To all women, I say: Do not give in to anything or anyone. Do not tolerate any corrupt government official or mafia criminal. Do not tolerate discrimination or mistreatment from anyone.

To the women of Olinalá, I ask that you continue the struggle that we began a year ago with our husbands and neighbors.

My captors are piling up charges against me. But I know that in the end I will walk out of this jail. I will do so with my head high because I know that no one believes that I am a criminal. There are honest people in Mexico, in the United States and other countries who know that I am a political prisoner.

I will leave prison to take up once again the struggle for community police that I initiated.

Onward, women of Mexico and the world! History teaches us that sacrifices are necessary to accomplish what we want. Let us stand fearless and determined to do away with evil and those who support it. This is how we women will build a bright and better future.

From the high security prison in Tepic, Nayarit

Three decades of class struggle on campus

Merle Woo

))) Without hesitation I can say that my 27-year career as a college lecturer was one long class struggle. Like any workplace, campuses have ugly competition, fights for benefits, raises and promotions, and betrayals by those seeking a piece of the managerial pie.

On one side are administrators and careerist tenured faculty members trying to maintain the status quo of education that benefits the ruling class. On the other side are progressive lecturers, staff, students, community activists and some tenured faculty.

I was engaged in a fight over students' minds, hearts and bodies. One of my major goals was to help students realize that the debased position of people of color, women, and queers in American society is used to justify the bosses' super-exploitation of us for profits. I wanted them to understand that the real focus of capitalist educational institutions is to maintain conformity and oppression. I wanted to help them grow into empowered individuals who, by working collaboratively, could find ways to transform this dehumanizing and degrading system.

Third World student strikes

In 1968-69, students, faculty, and community activists of color led militant Third World strikes across U.S. campuses. They won Ethnic Studies, affirmative action, the Educational Opportunity Program (EOP), student participation in decision-making, the hiring of activist faculty, and community-related courses. High school students of color were recruited to attend college, where they had never expected to find themselves.

In the Fall of 1969, I was hired to teach English for the EOP at San Francisco State. We teachers were a diverse group: Chicana, Black, Chinese American, American Indian, white working-class, and me, a Chinese-Korean American.

Class rivalries fractured relations in the program, showing me the false unity of alliances based solely on race.

At that time, I had not read anything by a Black writer or an Asian American writer. I had gotten all the way through a graduate program in English literature and never heard of Ralph Ellison. Such discoveries radicalized all the lecturers.

We couldn't find anything about people of color at the college bookstore. So we went out into our respective communities to record oral histories of our elders and works by new poets.

We taught our students that standard English was a dialect and proficiency at it — though necessary — had nothing to do with intelligence. Black English, Cantonese English, Spanglish — we gave the language color.

These were heady times. Asian Americans and women of color were fighting their way into visibility. There was pure joy in seeing formerly subservient Asian American students become authoritative, inquisitive, and angry.

But the take-backs began immediately. One or more EOP lecturers were terminated each year. At the end of each semester I had to go in to the Dean's office and make sure my courses, such as "Third World Literature" and "Lesbianism: An International Perspective," would be on the schedule the next term.

The fight in Asian American Studies

In the spring of 1978, I was hired as a full-time lecturer in Asian American Studies (AAS) at University of California - Berkeley. I was also teaching in the new Women Studies Department at San Francisco State. I felt like I had found myself — a proud Asian American feminist and mother, a writer, a lesbian, and a member of Radical Women and the Freedom Socialist Party.

It took a year to realize that all was not well in AAS. Long-time lecturers were leveling animosity at me (not the administration) because I had been hired in a position above them. Class rivalries fractured the relations of Asian Americans in the program, showing me the false unity of cultural nationalism — alliances based solely on race.

In my second year, I supported students by writing a letter protesting the elimination of community-language courses in Cantonese and Tagalog. AAS faculty were discontinuing community-related classes due to pressure to make the department more academic. My letter turned tenure-track faculty against me.

Dissident students and teachers led a spirited teach-in and boycott of Asian American Studies. We educated on the history of Ethnic Studies and affirmative action. We wore red armbands saying "Save Asian American Studies." But the community-related courses were lost and several outspoken lecturers were fired.

During this time I was also involved with Unbound Feet, a collective of six Chinese American performance poets that included Nellie Wong, Kitty Tsui, Canyon Sam, Genny Lim, and Nancy Hom. We were together almost two years. Three of us were out lesbians. We received incredible support. But, in 1981, we split over going public about AAS faculty breaking a contract with our group. This split gave impetus to tenured faculty who hated my politics. I heard through the grapevine that my boss, Ling-Chi Wang, said of me, "All she cares about is her radical politics and her poetry readings."

My opponents spread dirty little rumors. They wanted to ruin my reputation as a teacher and principled activist. They were very upset when I spoke at the 1981 San Francisco Lesbian and Gay Pride Rally.

Political differences at the university reflect class lines. In every community, there is an *establishment*. This elite sits on grant boards. They control the direction of departments and movements. Their job is to keep the lid on rebellion.

My case against UC Berkeley

In my fourth year in Asian American Studies, UC passed a four-year limitation on visiting lecturers. And — surprise! — I discovered I had been secretly demoted from *full-time* lecturer to *visiting* lecturer and could be fired under the new rule.

Radical Women and the Freedom Socialist Party helped form the Merle Woo Defense Committee (MWDC). My union, the American Federation of Teachers, filed an unfair labor practice to challenge the four-year rule. We learned that I was the only one laid off by Berkeley due to the rule. In 1983, an Administrative Law Judge threw out the four-year rule and ordered UC to rehire me. UC refused.

Our next step was to file complaints in federal and state courts charging violation of my free speech rights and discrimination based on race, sex, sexuality and political ideology. Students, unionists, and community activists supported my case. But there was opposition too. Some Asians, women, and gays hated my radicalism. Some feminists were racist and some labor bureaucrats didn't see discrimination as a labor issue. But we refused to compromise on any of the issues or to be limited by an identity politics approach. This was our strength.

The MWDC drew 20 staunch allies who did research, organized support and wrote briefs. Hundreds of well-known activists, academics, writers, even mainstream Democrats, endorsed the case.

Our legal briefs addressed the politics of the case head-on. We explained how socialist feminist politics are protected by the First Amendment and how democratically run educational programs benefit students and the community.

In the spring of 1982, a longtime AAS lecturer agreed to testify that Ling-Chi Wang had said, "It is inappropriate for a lesbian to represent Asian American Studies." That clinched our victory!

I was reinstated in 1984 at UC Berkeley.

Back to UC — and another battle

Though AAS wouldn't hire me, I taught in the Graduate School of Education. I was the faculty supervisor for anti-racist and lesbian/gay groups and joined Lesbians and Gays against Apartheid.

But in the spring of 1986, I was fired again — this time under the ruse that money had run out in a special fund that was paying me. This violated the mandate that all UC lecturers receive equal treatment. The Merle Woo Defense Committee filed a union grievance. It took three years — until 1989 — to get to arbitration.

Nearly 60 people attended the hearing. Unionists from the California Faculty Association and lecturers from San Francisco State crossed the Bay to support me. We won! The arbitrator ruled that I had been treated unfairly and was to be immediately reinstated.

From 1989 to 1991, I tried to get rehired at various departments.

UC hired a San Francisco law firm to block me. They

tried to drag me in for a psychiatric examination. We fought this outrageous demand and won. The judge said if UC played any more nasty acts of intimidation, she'd impose economic sanctions.

By 1991, however, we decided to drop the fight for reinstatement. I had just had a double mastectomy, and I wasn't about to be in litigation until I died.

Although never rehired at UC Berkeley, I won *three legal victories* against them, including back pay awards, setting important precedents for *the right to employment* for radicals, queers, feminists and unionists.

Report card

After three decades of struggle, the cutbacks and politics in education have only gotten worse. This is inevitable because we are still living under the same for-profit system.

But we have tasted freedom: there is no doubt that every student who has been involved in activism has been changed by exerting individual power in solidarity with others. Some have decided to devote their lives to organizing for a better world.

Political engagement is not difficult when we can envision what education would be like under socialism, where every child would enjoy quality education, where students would learn to think critically and speak out. And where each individual could choose to do something they love: from each according to ability, to each according to need.

CONTRIBUTORS

Farouk Abdel-Muhti
Palestinian exile and activist held without charges in U.S. prisons for nearly two years. He died in 2004, three months after being released. (pg. 142)

Yolanda Alaniz
Coordinator of Los Angeles Comrades of Color Caucus, retired archivist/librarian, co-author of *Viva La Raza: A History of Chicano Identity and Resistance.* (pg. 33, 77, 126)

Karla Alegria
Technical support worker, queer Salvadoran immigrant raised in Los Angeles, and organizer in defense of Nestora Salgado. (pg. 167)

Christine Browning
Chicana feminist and poet working for women's rights, the environment, and indigenous peoples; a lifelong learner. (pg. 187)

Mark Cook
Former Black Panther, imprisoned for 27 years in "20 different gulags" across the United States. Champion for rights of prisoners and labor. (pg. 50, 59)

Chris Faatz
Poetry lover, independent socialist, bookstore worker, and proud member of the International Longshore and Warehouse Union. (pg. 120)

Norma Gallegos
Bay Area Radical Women Organizer, public school worker, queer Chicana and San Francisco native. (pg. 92)

Yuisa Gimeno
Boston-born queer Puerto Rican, Los Angeles Radical Women Organizer, daughter of a Mexicana/Salvadoreña mover and shaker. (pg. 20, 84)

Maya Gonzalez
Guatemalan feminist and revolutionary. Fighter for immigrant

workers' rights; advocate for women and children against global capitalist exploitation. (pg. 139)

John Hatchett
Professor and campus civil rights leader in the early 1960s, then a teacher, writer and Harlem community organizer. He died in 2009. (pg. 107)

Nancy Reiko Kato
Union leader and campus firebrand at the University of California; stalwart organizer for reproductive rights. (pg. 97, 123, 197)

Christina López
Arizona native, FSP candidate for U.S. Vice-President in 2012, defender of immigrant rights, leader in campaign to free Nestora Salgado. (pg. 175, 192, 203, 210)

Moisés Montoya
Bay Area Chicano gay radical, Oakland public employee and unionist, participant in Berkeley anti-apartheid and Occupy Wall Street movements. (pg. 161)

Hugo Orellana
Originally from Guatemala; survived the harrowing journey through the U.S. immigration system; now a U.S. citizen, public employee and union member. (pg. 71, 81)

Miriam Padilla
College student and single mother; organizing to free Nestora Salgado; aspires to become a social justice attorney. (pg. 89)

Noel Perez
Communications tech and member of Communications Workers of America. After a two-year wait, his wife received a visa to join him in Los Angeles from Mexico. (pg. 74)

Ralph Poynter
Radical Black community activist; advocate for the release of his wife, political prisoner Lynne Stewart, and all prisoners of an unjust system. (pg. 170)

Ann Rogers
Anti-Nazi fighter and Native American movement veteran of Chippewa ancestry. Retired Teamster Local 130 shop steward and grandmother. (pg. 158, 184)

Nestora Salgado
U.S. citizen imprisoned in Mexico for her leadership of an indigenous community police force in her home village of Olinalá, Guerrero. (pg. 220)

Sarah Scott
Prideful African American; a restaurant worker by day, a creative writer, fashion designer and socialist feminist by night. (pg. 117)

Lillian Thompson
Born and raised in South Central Los Angeles, African American elementary school teacher and fighter for bilingual education. (pg. 29)

Duciana Thomas
African American feminist and writer. Graduate of Mills College with a B.A. in Women's, Gender and Sexuality Studies. Works for survivors of domestic abuse. (pg. 15)

Annaliza Torres
Pinay (Filipina American) social services provider, member of Office and Professional Employees International Union Local 8 in Seattle. (pg. 25, 133)

Nellie Wong
Groundbreaking Asian American feminist poet, author of four volumes of poetry; past organizer for the Freedom Socialist Party. (pg. 7, 45, 129)

Merle Woo
Korean-Chinese American lesbian poet, retired lecturer in Women and Asian American Studies. Won landmark discrimination battles against University of California. (pg. 102, 112, 225)

Emily Woo Yamasaki
Chair of the National Comrades of Color Caucus, queer feminist, and New York City organizer for Radical Women. (pg. 55, 180)

INDEX

Red Letter Press

REVOLUTIONARY INTEGRATION:
A Marxist Analysis of African American Liberation
by Richard Fraser and Tom Boot
Groundbreaking study of the Black struggle, the nature of racism, and the ongoing fight for Freedom Now. **$17.95**

VIVA LA RAZA:
A History of Chicano Identity and Resistance
by Yolanda Alaniz and Megan Cornish
A riveting account of the struggle for Chicana/o liberation that reveals the workings of race and nationality in the U.S. **$19.00**

SOCIALIST FEMINISM AND THE REVOLUTIONARY PARTY
by Andrea Bauer
In-depth look at why Marxist feminism, embodied in a revolutionary party, is a radiant program for new generations. **$5.00**

WOMEN OF COLOR:
Front-runners for Freedom
by Nancy Reiko Kato
Analyzes how women of color are destined to lead the coming socialist feminist revolution. Radical Women pamphlet. **$3.50**

THE RADICAL WOMEN MANIFESTO:
Socialist Feminist Theory, Program and Organizational Structure
An exhilarating exploration of ideas and an unrivaled guide to activism from a groundbreaking feminist organization. **$8.00**
Spanish edition $5.00

Order from Red Letter Press
4710 University Way NE #100, Seattle, WA 98105
Telephone: (206)985-4621 • Fax (206)985-8965
RedLetterPress@juno.com • www.RedLetterPress.org